National and State Banks

*This is a volume
in the Arno Press collection*

THE RISE OF COMMERCIAL BANKING

Advisory Editors
Stuart W. Bruchey
Vincent P. Carosso

*See last pages of this volume
for a complete list of titles.*

National and State Banks

A STUDY OF THEIR ORIGINS

linton

LEONARD C. HELDERMAN

ARNO PRESS

A New York Times Company
New York • 1980

Editorial Supervision: **Doris Krone**

———

Reprint Edition 1980 by Arno Press Inc.

Reprinted from a copy in The University of Michigan Library

THE RISE OF COMMERCIAL BANKING

ISBN for complete set: 0-405-13626-9
See last pages of this volume for titles.

Manufactured in the United States of America

———

Library of Congress Cataloging in Publication Data

Helderman, Leonard Clinton.
  National and state banks.

  (The Rise of commercial banking)
  Reprint of the 1931 ed. published by Houghton
Mifflin, Boston, which was issued as v. 49 of
series: Hart, Schaffner & Marx prize essays.
  Originally presented as the author's thesis,
University of Wisconsin--Madison, 1929.
  Bibliography: p.
  1. Banks and banking--United States--History.
2. National banks (United States)--History.
I. Title. II. Series: Rise of commercial banking
III. Series: Hart, Schaffner & Marx prize
essays ; 49.
HG2461.H4 1980   332.1'22'0973   80-1149
ISBN 0-405-13652-8

𝕳art, 𝕾chaffner & 𝕸arx 𝕻rize 𝕰ssays

XLIX

NATIONAL AND STATE BANKS
A STUDY OF THEIR ORIGINS

National and State Banks

A STUDY OF THEIR ORIGINS

BY

LEONARD C. HELDERMAN

Associate Professor of History, Washington and Lee University

BOSTON AND NEW YORK
HOUGHTON MIFFLIN COMPANY
The Riverside Press Cambridge
1931

The Riverside Press
CAMBRIDGE · MASSACHUSETTS
PRINTED IN THE U.S.A.

TO MY WIFE
HAZEL RINKARD HELDERMAN

PREFACE

THIS series of books owes its existence to the generosity of Messrs. Hart, Schaffner & Marx, of Chicago, who have desired to encourage a wider interest in the study of economic and commercial subjects. For this purpose they have delegated to the undersigned committee the task of selecting or approving of topics, making announcements, and awarding prizes annually for those who wish to compete.

For the year 1929 there were offered:

In Class A, which included any American without restriction, a first prize of $1000, and a second prize of $500.

In Class B, which included any who were at the time undergraduates of an American college, a first prize of $300, and a second prize of $200.

Any essay submitted in Class B, if deemed of sufficient merit, could receive a prize in Class A.

The present volume, submitted in Class A, was awarded Second Prize in 1929.

J. LAURENCE LAUGHLIN, *Chairman*
University of Chicago
JOHN B. CLARK
Columbia University
EDWIN F. GAY
Washington, D.C.
WESLEY C. MITCHELL
Columbia University

AUTHOR'S PREFACE

THIS study was undertaken on the suggestion of Professor C. R. Fish, of the University of Wisconsin, completed under his direction, and accepted as a doctor's thesis in June, 1929. To his sympathetic criticism and broad humanism the author must acknowledge a paramount obligation. An especial debt is due, moreover, to Professor F. L. Paxson, of the University of Wisconsin, for reading the manuscript and for the high privilege which the author had of attending his brilliant lectures. The portions dealing with western finance are deeply marked by his influence. The chapter on the Old South owes much to Dean C. S. Boucher, of the University of Chicago, in whose seminar it was pursued, and to Professor U. B. Phillips, of Yale, who criticized the chapter in an early stage of preparation. Professor William E. Dodd, of the University of Chicago, gave valuable assistance on the repudiation movement in Mississippi, as did also the late Professor F. L. Riley, of Washington and Lee University.

This study has been fortunate in having the attention of a group of economists, the Committee of the Hart, Schaffner, and Marx Economic Prize contest: Professors J. L. Laughlin, E. F. Gay, J. B. Clark, W. C. Mitchell, and the late Senator Theodore Burton. That eminent student of economic history, Professor Gay, of Harvard, gave the final proof a close reading. His careful editing smoothed out many places in an all too rough piece of work. The author has had access to the unfailing courtesy and critical attention of Dr. John Cummings, of the Research Division of the Federal Reserve Board. Under his supervision the manuscript was revised and expanded. He has saved the author many an error in dealing with such a highly technical subject as finance. Dean G. D. Hancock, of the School of Commerce and Business Administration at Washington and Lee University, read and offered valuable criticism on Chapters VII and VIII. This imposing array of historical and economic talent, however, cannot relieve the author of responsibility for errors of fact and mistaken viewpoint.

Secretary Chase, in recommending the National Banking System, said that his proposal was not an 'untried theory,' but that it was based on practical experience. This volume covers, in the main, the experience which Chase had in mind. Chapter I deals with the panic of 1837 in its international aspect; Chapters II–V are devoted to the experience of selected States; Chapter VI considers the problem of the immediate origins of the National Banking System during the Civil War; Chapter VII is a summary of the origins of technical principles; and Chapter VIII considers some of the later influence of early State experience. Some data will doubtless appear as having little direct bearing on the National System and at points to go beyond it to later American financial history. The National System, however, is the main objective and will be seen to emerge from the experience covered.

It should be noted that all State bank experience before the Civil War is not considered. Several systems, notably those of Pennsylvania, Virginia, and Maryland, are omitted; and many matters which will readily suggest themselves to the student are not fully covered. A complete history of ante-bellum State banking would include the systems of all the States as well as such matters as the panic of 1857; the rôle of European capital; the effect of repudiation on the bond deposit systems and on the general credit in Europe; and the experience of the bond deposit systems in relation to the extinction of the national debt, the limitation of State debts, and the business cycle.

This volume is not designed as a manual for the practical banker. It is a study in economic history. The economist in reading an historical dissertation frequently feels that it is an antiquarian essay, bristling with formidable footnotes pointing toward and signifying nothing. Many historians would not only concede the point but applaud it. But many monographs, deadly as they are, must precede interpretation. The historian, moreover, in reading a technical treatise misses a recognition of the principles of comparative growth and continuity.

L. C. HELDERMAN

LEXINGTON, VIRGINIA

CONTENTS

NATIONAL AND STATE BANKS
A STUDY OF THEIR ORIGINS

CHAPTER I

THE FINANCIAL CRISIS OF THE THIRTIES

THE Second United States Bank expired on March 3, 1836, by limitation of charter and by the will of Andrew Jackson. It had been a bitter but a bloodless seven years' bank war. Ever since he had read of the South Sea Bubble, Jackson had been 'afraid of banks' — not merely the United States Bank, but all paper money banks. He, like many of his day, was a 'hard money man,' thinking that paper money was not only unconstitutional but bad policy. When he became President in 1829 his views had not changed except that he had become suspicious of the Second United States Bank as a monopoly and a corrupt influence. But the man whose temper has become proverbial knew how to conceal an iron hand within a velvet glove. He did not speak the hostile words he had written for the inaugural of March, 1829. But his mind was made up and he spoke it in the first annual message of December — mild words, indeed, edited by the son of Alexander Hamilton. As Clay and Biddle pressed the fight in the succeeding years, Jackson's temper rose and his words had the sharp tone of the battlefield. When in March, 1837, the retiring President gave his farewell warning to the nation, the war was over. The charter had been vetoed, the deposits removed, the Specie Circular issued, the censure expunged, and Nicholas Biddle had for a year and a day taken sanctuary for his 'monster' in a Pennsylvania charter. Yet commercial distress already hovered in the offing — two months and the panic of 1837 was upon the nation. The Whigs said Jackson was the cause — a bull in the china shop of sound money. And it was true enough that the war on the Bank had weakened its regulating power, the Specie Circular had drained reserves from state banks, and the panic of May had followed hard on the farewell address of March. Yet there was coincidence in these events as well as cause. It is necessary to note that other factors were involved in the crisis.

The expansion period of the thirties and the financial crisis which climaxed the decade are not to be viewed as originating solely in American events. The business cycle was a world phenomenon, aggravated in America by such particular circumstances as land speculation, internal improvements, manufacturing development, and the economic revolution in the cotton South. It is difficult to suppose that a rechartered and unmolested United States Bank could have prevented either the expansion or the panic. It must be noted that it possessed no control over the discount rate such as the Bank of England exercised and for a debtor nation such a power would have been difficult to employ. The principle was little understood, if at all, and was never effectively applied until America ceased to be a debtor nation.[1]

---

[1] American economic history has stressed the factors of land and labor but has devoted little attention to the equally important matter of migrating capital. Virtually all the bonded debts of the American States had been contracted since 1820, and the largest amount since 1830. Senator Hubbard placed the total bonded debt for 1838 at about $174,-000,000 — figures based on information collected by the New York Comptroller of the Currency. Of this total, $148,000,000 had been contracted since 1830 and $108,000,000 since 1835 (*Congressional Globe*, 26th Cong., 1st Sess., VIII, p. 198, February 18, 1840). A detailed analysis of State debts made by the Treasury Department in 1842, placed the total in excess of $207,000,000 (*Letter from the Secretary of the Treasury on Debts of the Several States*, June 25, 1842, in 27th Cong., 2d Sess., *House Ex. Doc.* No. 254). These figures are merely the bonded debts of States and Territories and omit such matters as debts of cities, corporations, and individuals — items which would materially swell the total. How much of the total represented European capital invested in America is a point about which it is impossible to be exact. A committee of the Missouri Legislature in 1838 estimated the total foreign debt at $125,-000,000 (25th Cong., 3d Sess., *House Ex. Doc.* No. 227, p. 604, Nov. 20, 1838). President Van Buren in 1839 said: 'The foreign debt of our States, corporations, and men of business can scarcely be less than $200,000,000' (Richardson, III, p. 552, December 2, 1839). On this problem see also: R. W. Dunn, *American Foreign Investments* (New

The crisis must also be viewed in relation to such economic currents in Europe as the rapid industrial development after Waterloo, the export of surplus capital to the high interest areas of new lands, and to the world-wide cotton industry, transforming in Lancashire looms the raw material of the southern plantation into the finished product aboard an East India clipper. These new economic forces were no respecters of nationalism or particularism. They had an inherent natural logic more relentless than the arguments of Calhoun and Webster. In the international credit structure created by these forces the Bank of England occupied a central position and its bullion reserve was a barometer. 'The nineteenth century credit system,' says a recent writer, 'is not to be interpreted as consisting of a number of countries each exercising independent control over credit within its own limits.... It is rather to be regarded as a centralized system responding to a leader. The center was London and the leader the Bank of England.' [1]

As a symptom of the world-wide nature of the expansion, the bullion reserves of the great London institution fell from 10,900,000 to 4,300,000 pounds sterling between October 1, 1833, and December 27, 1836. The most threatening specie drain occurred in 1836 — 2,600,000 pounds sterling between April and September, of which 2,300,000 were 'supposed to have been exported to America.' [2] The Bank of England became alarmed at this movement, and in June, 1836, raised the discount rate from four to four and one half per cent,

York, 1926); C. K. Hobson, *Export of Capital* (New York, 1914); L. H. Jenks, *The Migration of British Capital* (New York, 1927); and *The International Financial Position of the United States* (New York, 1929), the latter a publication of the National Industrial Conference Board.

[1] R. G. Hawtrey, 'London and the Trade Cycle,' in *American Economic Review*, Supplement, XIX (1929).

[2] J. Horsely Palmer, *The Causes and Consequences of the Pressure upon the Money Market* (London, 1837), pp. 12; 23; 29. The author was ex-governor of the Bank of England and a prominent director from 1811 to 1857. This pamphlet was written either in December, 1836, or early in 1837. A reply to it by Samuel Lloyd Jones (later Lord Overstone) is dated February, 1837. This controversy between Palmer and Jones is reviewed in *Edinburgh Review*, LXV (April, 1837), pp. 61–87.

and to five per cent in August.[1] Besides raising the discount rate the Bank of England in September, 1836, employed another weapon of contraction by ordering its Liverpool agent 'to reject the paper of certain American Houses,' as the agencies of American firms were called. These firms followed the practice of buying in England on four months paper which had ordinarily been discounted by the Bank of England. By March 1, 1837, the three largest American firms suspended payment on over 5,000,000 pounds sterling of their acceptances.[2] There can be little question as to the effect of this contraction policy on American specie reserves. Specie exportation from England to America ceased by September, 1836, and Palmer thought it 'not improbable that we may soon see it return from that quarter of the world.'[3] Several prominent Englishmen, moreover, gave testimony bearing on this point before the House of Commons in 1840,[4] and English and Continental writers were

[1] *Annual Register* (1837), pp. 171–74.

[2] 'The Crisis in the American Trade,' in *Edinburgh Review*, LXV (July, 1837), pp. 221–38; *Annual Register* (1837), pp. 182–84; *North American Review* (January, 1844), article by B. R. Curtis.

[3] J. Horsely Palmer, *The Causes and Consequences of the Pressure upon the Money Market*, pp. 23; 32. Some thought the rate should have been raised as high as seven per cent. Palmer wrote: 'We must keep in mind that England is the centre of the whole commerce of Europe and America, if not the world, and any hasty or unnecessary step taken, will not only affect the credit and prices of this country, but to a certain degree, those of all parts of the Continent....'

[4] *Report from the Select Committee on Banks of Issue*, August 7, 1840. The President of the Manchester Chamber of Commerce, J. B. Smith, said that the Bank had been obliged 'to raise its rate of interest... and at the same time to reduce its loans by rejecting all bills drawn by joint stock banks of issue and bills drawn upon the Anglo-American houses. The result of these measures was great commercial embarrassment and general discredit, both in this and in foreign countries...' (pp. 2–3). Richard Cobden saw the cause of the panic in the action of the Bank 'at the end of 1836 in striking a blow at the American houses, and in advancing the rate of interest.' He considered the increase of the rate a proper and necessary measure, but thought it came too late. The Bank, said he, had no sooner announced its rule of a 'full currency' — a reserve of one third — than it violated it (p. 35; see also *London Bankers' Magazine*, I, pp. 14 ff.). Thomas Tooke thought that the proper method to stop a foreign drain was to increase the rate (pp. 356–57). In 1839 a more serious drain began. Bullion which in January, 1839, stood well above

commonly aware of the factor during the nineteenth century. Among those who called attention to the international aspect of the panic and its relation to America were: Thomas Tooke,[1] Alexander Trotter,[2] Clement Juglar,[3] Max Wirth,[4] Michael von Tugan Baranowski,[5] and others.[6] Count D'Argout, Governor of the Bank of France, understood the situation as early as January, 1837.[7] Moreover, some alert persons in America were aware of these factors both before and after the panic of 1837.

9,000,000 pounds sterling sank to a record low level of 2,500,000 by October 15. In the face of this movement the Bank adopted heroic measures. The discount rate which in 1838 had been as low as three and one half per cent was progressively advanced to five per cent on May 16; to five and one half per cent on June 20; and to the 'unprecedented rate' of six per cent on August 1, 1839. By October the drain had ceased, and bullion began to flow back into the vaults of the Bank. (Testimony of G. W. Norman and J. H. Palmer, pp. 118–20; 156–57).

[1] Thomas Tooke, *A History of Prices* (London, 1840), pp. 73 ff. He discusses the pressures of 1836 and 1839. One of the causes of the low reserve in 1836 was: 'the excessive credits to the United States of America....'

[2] Alexander Trotter, *Observations on the Financial Position and Credit of Such States of the North American Union as have contracted Public Debts* (London, 1839), pp. 41–43.

[3] Clement Juglar, *A Brief History of Panics and their Periodical Occurrence in the United States* (New York, 1893), translated by D. W. Thom, p. 66 — 'The advance in the discount rate in the Bank of England... came like a thunder clap and the distended bladder burst.'

[4] Max Wirth, *Geschichte der Handelskrisen* (Frankfort, 1874), pp. 181–85.

[5] Michael von Tugan Baranowski, *Studien zur Theorie und Geschichte der Handelskrisen in England* (Jena, 1901), pp. 86–93. He emphasizes the flow of capital to America for development purposes, the fall of reserves in London, and the contraction policy of the Bank of England.

[6] James William Gilbart, *The History of Banking in America* (London, 1837), pp. 143 ff.; John Francis, *History of the Bank of England* (2 vols., London, 1848), II, pp. 97, 118; D. M. Evans, *The History of the Commercial Crisis, 1857–58, and the Stock Exchange Panic of 1859* (London, 1859), pp. 5–7; 18–20.

[7] *The Financial Register of the United States* I, p. 89 — a short-lived periodical edited at Philadelphia by Condy Raguet. The Governor of the Bank of France, in his statement of January 26, 1837, also called attention to the fact that the Bank of Amsterdam had followed the Bank of England in advancing the discount rate. Although there was a great drain on the Bank of France, it did not advance the rate.

Nicholas Biddle, while disposed to see the trouble in what a recent student has termed 'Jackson's ferocious attack on the United States Bank';[1] nevertheless appears to have understood that something was happening in Europe. In November, 1836, he wrote: 'While Europe is alarmed, and the Bank of England itself uneasy at the quantity of specie we possess, we are suffering because, from mere mismanagement, the whole ballast of the currency is shifted from one side of the vessel to the other.'[2] A. J. Colcock, President of the Bank of the State of South Carolina, was also aware of the omens. 'The late difficulties,' he wrote in 1836, 'between the Bank of England and the American Merchants have developed some important and startling facts, which are worthy of serious consideration, when we advert to the standing which is held by that great institution.... Added to the universal increase in the commerce of the world, arising from the peaceful state of Europe and America for the last thirty years, the rapid use and improvement of the latter have required and exhausted no small amount of the capital of England, and, consequently, their operations at present are somewhat contracted.... The truths of these facts have been greatly felt during the last year, and are at this moment operating in our community, and it will require all the aid of a good crop to afford relief to us and assistance to them. So much specie has been drawn from England of late, that every effort must now be made by her to prevent a further drain, and interest has risen in every part of Europe, as far as we can obtain information.'[3] Edmond J. Forstall, prominent financier of New Orleans and President of the Citizens' Bank, saw the same signs. As agent for Baring Brothers and Hope and Company, he was in touch with the money market of Lombard Street; and as early as September, 1836, was importing specie from Havana and Mexico to strengthen the

---

[1] R. G. McGrane, *The Panic of 1837* (Chicago, 1924), p. 183. This is the most recent study of the panic of 1837 and views it largely from the domestic angle.

[2] Trotter, pp. 39–40.

[3] 24th Cong., 2d Sess., *House Ex. Doc.* No. 65, pp. 139–40. This report is undated, but bears internal evidence of being written before the close of 1836, perhaps the annual report of December.

reserves of New Orleans. In February, 1837, moreover, in a famous report to the Louisiana legislature which became the basis of the powerful system of 1842, he called attention to the policy started by the Bank of England in June, 1836, 'with a view, by contracting suddenly their business to force the exportation of gold and silver from the United States to replenish their empty vaults.'[1] Samuel Merril, President of the State Bank of Indiana, which by virtue of the river trade had large dealings with New Orleans, saw the same portents. He attributed the tightening money market at the close of 1836 to a decrease in specie imports from Mexico, the suppression of small bills, the Specie Circular, and the restrictive action of the Bank of England.[2] The Secretary of the Treasury called attention to the sharp fall in the price of cotton in 1836, the shrinkage of reserves in England, and added that 'an alarm and pressure have arisen there, which are operating unfavorably here....'[3]

Important, but perhaps less significant, were the statements made after the panic. The Secretary of the Treasury noted a great shrinkage in exports, 'occasioned chiefly by the great fall in the price of cotton during the last spring.'[4] Charles Francis Adams noted that the bubble burst at the great cotton export center of New Orleans. He wrote: 'On that day [March 4] happened at New Orleans the first great commercial bankruptcy, the precursor of the general suspension of specie payments in May.... The inducing cause was the recall of capital borrowed from Europe.'[5] The Bank Commissioners of New York summarized the causes of the panic as follows: 'This reaction commenced by a sudden check given to American credit in Europe, which threw back a large amount of protested bills, and created a large and

[1] 25th Cong., 2d Sess., *House Ex. Doc.* No. 79, pp. 609–20; 651–53. For information that Forstall was agent at New Orleans for European firms, this study is indebted to his granddaughter, Mother Saint Helen (Forstall) of the Ursuline Convent, New Orleans.

[2] *Ibid.*, pp. 785–86, December 16, 1836.

[3] *Annual Report of the Secretary of the Treasury*, December 6, 1836, in 24th Cong., 2d Sess., *House Ex. Doc.* No. 4.

[4] *Ibid.*, December 6, 1837, in 24th Cong., 2d Sess., *Sen. Doc.* No. 2.

[5] Charles Francis Adams, *Further Reflections on the Currency* (Boston, 1837).

threatening demand for specie to export, which immediately raised it to a premium, while the same causes operated to depress the great staple of the country in the market abroad, and render in a great measure unavailable the only means of remittance actually possessed, except the stock of specie. The immediate cause of the *run* upon the banks... was this foreign demand for specie.' [1] This factor was alluded to also by President Van Buren,[2] Henry Clay,[3] Benjamin R. Curtis,[4] Governor Roman of Louisiana,[5] Governor Marcy of New York,[6] the Louisiana Board of Currency,[7] the Massachusetts Bank Commissioners,[8] and others.[9] It is not clear, however, that these persons in America understood the principle of the discount rate, but it is certain that the principle did not cease to operate with the panic of 1837.[10]

[1] 25th Cong., 2d Sess., *Sen. Doc.* No. 471, p. 791, January 24, 1836.

[2] J. D. Richardson, *Messages and Papers of the Presidents* (10 vols. Washington, 1896), III, p. 327, September 4, 1837; III, p. 545, December 2, 1839.

[3] 27th Cong., 1st Sess., *Senate Doc.* No 32, pp. 5–6. Clay in submitting a report June 21, 1841, regarding the Fiscal Bank said: 'We have seen the influence exerted by the Bank of England upon American interests, when those interests were exposed to the action of that bank, and were left without the protection of the Bank of the United States.'

[4] *Life and Writings of Benjamin R. Curtis* (2 vols. Boston, 1879), II, pp. 93–148. This is an elaborate and able presentation of the view that the panic originated in Europe, particularly in England.

[5] 26th Cong., 2d Sess., *House Ex. Doc.* No. 111, p. 631, January, 1840.

[6] *Niles' Register*, LIV, p. 130, April 12, 1838.

[7] *Louisiana House Journal* (1844), Appendix.

[8] *Mass. Public Documents* (1865), III, p. 38.

[9] A committee of the Missouri Legislature in 25th Cong., 3d Sess., *House Ex. Doc.* No. 227, pp. 604–05; the directors of an Ohio bank in 25th Cong., 2d Sess., *Senate Doc.* No. 471, pp. 393–94; and the *Democratic Review*, March, 1838, pp. 381–402.

[10] The same symptoms of expansion are visible in England in the period after 1850. With a bullion reserve in the Bank of England amounting to 22,000,000 pounds sterling and a discount rate of two per cent, English capital flowed into American enterprise. By 1856, reserves had shrunk to 9,500,000 pounds sterling and the interest rate was raised to seven per cent. The Governor of the Bank of England testified before the House of Commons that the cause of the drain was a foreign demand and that an advance of the discount rate was the method employed to restore the reserves. *Report from the Select Committee on Bank Acts*, July 30, 1857, p. 31; Appendix No. 15.

The precise influence of these factors is, of course, not susceptible of scientific demonstration. If the evidence is not sufficient to warrant the definitive conclusion that the primary cause was the contraction policy of the Bank of England, it is sufficient to provoke the question: Has the panic not been viewed too narrowly as an American phenomenon — as a simple result, indeed, of Jacksonian policy? Altogether it may fairly be said that the panic resulted from a combination of these causes. Whatever the cause the result was clear.

The panic of 1837 left the American banking system virtually a wreck. Under the lash of economic distress two clear tendencies emerged: one, a reform movement; the other, a sharp anti-bank reaction. The reform movement first evolved a program in New York where in 1838 the free-bank system was created. This, gradually perfected by a quarter century of experience in New York, and imitated by other States, became the model of the National System of 1863. A contemporary reform movement in the cotton export center of New Orleans, although delayed until 1842, resulted in a powerful system. This, tested by the panic of 1857, vitally influenced the National System. Another result of the panic of 1837 was to intensify the hard money ideas of the day, leading to a movement in the West to abolish banks of issue. This movement subsided before the rising business cycle of the fifties, and, absurd as it may seem today, was based on a theory shared by many sober men of the time.

The field of this study lies principally in the quarter century which separates the passing of the Second United States Bank from the beginning of the Civil War. It is difficult, however, to erect an inviolable time limit, for systems were in existence at the time of the panic and must be placed against their historic backgrounds. This will necessitate, in many cases, reaching back some years before the panic. This period is conceived to be one of constructive banking legislation — a period of growth not of decay. It is the creative age of Jacksonian Democracy — the hunting ground for origins of many enduring features of later American society. It is here that many State systems as well as the National Banking System directly root. To some extent, more-over, the present Federal Reserve System may be thought of as indirectly reaching back into the period of State experience.

CHAPTER II

ORGANIZED SYSTEMS OF THE EAST

THE SAFETY-FUND SYSTEM OF NEW YORK

At the time of the panic of 1837, the banking system of New York consisted of three types of issue banks. There were the so-called 'perpetual charter' banks; i.e., the Manhattan Company, and the Dry Docks. The former had been organized in 1799 by Aaron Burr to supply New York City with water, the latter had been originally designed, as the name implies, for a drydock. These held charters without time limitations from which they 'implied' banking privileges. The second type were those chartered for definite banking purposes and with definite time limits in their charters. These were created by special legislative acts between 1791 and 1829, the oldest being Hamilton's Bank of North America. The third type were members of the Safety-Fund System, to which attention will first be directed.[1]

The Safety-Fund System, adopted in 1829, was an attempt to introduce a more closely organized system and provide more protection for circulation. It aimed to include all banks of the State upon the expiration of the existing charters. For administrative purposes a board of three commissioners was created; one appointed by the Governor and representing the State, and two others appointed by city and

[1] *Report of the Comptroller of the Currency*, December 30, 1848, in New York *Assembly Documents*, 1849, I, No. 5, p. 34. This report was made by Millard Fillmore, who was Comptroller of the New York Currency, from January 1, 1848, to February 20, 1849. It is not only a brilliant defense of the New York principle, but sketches the early history of banking in the State. Moreover, it contains a significant suggestion of a National currency based on the New York idea. This document will also be found in 31st Cong., 1st Sess., *House Ex. Doc.* No. 68; and in the Buffalo Historical Society *Publications*, X, pp. 275–83. *The Report of the Superintendent of Banks*, January, 1857, in 34th Cong., 3d Sess., *House Ex. Doc.* No. 87, reviews New York bank history from colonial times. A. R. Hasse, *Index... New York*, is an indispensable guide through the legislative documents.

rural banks. This board had power to inspect quarterly, and was required to examine any bank upon the request of any three member banks. The most important feature was the provision for a 'safety-fund' for the protection of notes issued. This fund consisted of annual contributions of member banks — each bank contributing one half per cent of its capital until its contributions amounted to three per cent of its capital. This common fund was controlled by the Commissioners, and 'inviolably appropriated to the payment of such portions of the debt, exclusive of capital stock, of any of the said corporations, which shall become insolvent.'[1]

The system was not popular with the city banks, at first, because they feared the principle of mutual liability in cases of insolvency. The New York City banks had usually restricted their issues below the legal maximum, but country banks were not so cautious and ordinarily held weak reserves. Moreover, the city banks insisted that the nature of business in New York City forced them to maintain high reserves, while competition with the branch of the United States Bank reduced interest rates and dividends. Nor were the objections of the city banks without reason, as the statistics of experience under the system show. With a circulation proportionally much lower, with loans more contracted, and with higher reserves, it was with reason that the city banks felt they were sharing the burdens of the system while the speculative profits went to the less cautious banks.[2]

Although the system operated successfully until 1837, the great number of failures in the panic made heavy drains on the three per cent fund. Out of eleven insolvent banks, two were finally able to meet their obligations from general assets without drawing on the common fund. The other nine, however, drew from the fund $2,565,334, and their assets realized but $133,077.[3] From this experience one serious de-

[1] New York, *Assembly Journal*, 1829, pp. 752–56. The most important exposition of the system is: R. E. Chaddock, 'Safety-Fund Banking System of New York,' in National Monetary Commission *Reports*, IV (1910); and a brief analysis is given by Albert Gallatin's *Suggestions* (1841).

[2] Chaddock, pp. 267–69; 296–97.

[3] *Ibid.*, p. 332.

fect was clear. The officials in charge of the fund accepted the interpretation that the fund could only be used for payment of balances due creditors after liquidation of general assets. This was a tedious process, ordinarily requiring several years to complete, and since a bank note depreciates unless promptly redeemed, billholders lost. It was estimated that losses from this source alone amounted to $350,000. To remedy this defect a law was passed directing the immediate application of the fund; reserving, however, one third of it for depositors.[1] This diversion was regarded by the Bank Commissioners as a defect. 'The Safety-Fund Act,' they said, 'was primarily designed to secure bank-note holders and not depositors and other creditors.... No man is bound to deposit in a bank unless he pleases, and if he voluntarily assumes in this manner, to make it his debtor, no good reason can be perceived, why he should be entitled to greater protection than that of the bank to which he gives credit.'[2] Such was the general opinion of bankers before 1857, for the deposit feature in banking was less important than the note issue until about 1855.

The fund proved inadequate for both deposit and note liability. In 1845, due to a deficit, 'bank fund bonds' to the amount of $900,000 were issued in anticipation of future additions to the fund. By 1848 the total contributions since 1829 amounted to $1,876,063; and from this $1,548,558 had been drawn for note redemption. The deficit, therefore, represented the amount of the fund diverted to deposit protection, and indicated that the fund would have proved ample for note protection.[3]

The safety-fund banks, chartered between 1829 and 1838, continued to exist until the National Banking System. No new charters were granted after 1838, for a new system took its place. It was superseded by the free-bank system,

[1] Chaddock, p. 302.

[2] *Annual Report of the Bank Commissioners*, January 23, 1841, in 26th Cong., 2d Sess., *House Ex. Doc.* No. 111, p. 131. It must be understood, however, that by the original act of 1829, noteholders were not made preferred creditors. The fund was for all creditors, which of course included depositors.

[3] *Report of the Comptroller of Currency*, December 30, 1848, in New York *Assembly Documents*, 1849, I, p. 116.

but the principle of a safety-fund continued to exert an influence long after the passing of the New York system. It exerted no influence on the National Bank Act, but it was adopted by Canada in 1890 with a larger fund and stronger safeguards.[1] Moreover, during the currency reform discussions following the panics of 1893 and 1907, the idea was revived and proposed in responsible quarters.[2]

TRANSITION TO FREE BANKING

The most important product of the period of State experimentation was the free-bank system of New York. This system of 1838 was of paramount importance, both because of its influence on the legislation of other States, and because it became the model for the National Banking System. Aside from the technical principle, it was the solution to the problem of how to secure financial stability without centralized monopoly. It became the compromise ground between the 'hard money' demand for the abolition of banks of issue, and the rigid Whig insistence on a Hamiltonian National Bank. As it passed into the National Banking System it avoided the objection which Jackson placed first in his Veto of July 10, 1832 — a point which Fillmore, Chase, and Hooper noted. Historically, in its English background, the idea of 'free banking' was a product of the theory of *laissez-faire*, even to the extent of allowing private individuals to issue bank notes, without any government regulation other than the common law rule of personal liability. It was this definition that Albert Gallatin had in mind when he wrote: 'By free banking, in its genuine sense, I understand the extension of that permission to all persons or associations of persons, free of all restraints, but on his or their personal responsibility.'[3] The fatal defect of such a theory was, of

[1] R. M. Breckenridge, 'History of Banking in Canada,' in National Monetary Commission *Reports*, IX (1910), p. 137.

[2] The 'Baltimore Plan' of the American Bankers' Association in 1894 proposed the substitution of a Guarantee Fund for the bond security principle, and the same proposal was made in 1907. *Journal of Political Economy*, III, pp. 101–05; Myron T. Herrick, 'The Panic of 1907 and its Lessons,' in *Annals, American Academy*, XXXI, pp. 16–19.

[3] Henry Adams, *Writings of Albert Gallatin* (3 vols., Philadelphia,

course, its conflict with social welfare — a mistaken view which led John Bright to oppose factory regulation, and Jeremy Bentham to favor repeal of all usury laws.[1] In America, however, free banking came to mean, not the removal of social control, but the removal of what was deemed special privilege, and a note issue protected by a deposit of securities with public officers. In regard to the first point; it will be remembered that under the Safety-Fund System, and indeed all systems of the Nation, bank charters could be secured only by special acts of the legislatures. It was against this practice that the anti-monopoly argument was directed. It was the first point of Jackson's argument in 1832, and came to be generally adopted in the 'Jacksonian constitutions' of the two decades following. Although Albert Gallatin took no stock in the more violent charges of Jackson and his group against the Second Bank, it seems

1880), III, pp. 563–64, Gallatin to A. C. Flagg, December 31, 1841. Gallatin, of course, was not in favor of such a system, for note issue.

[1] New York *Senate Documents*, 1837, I, No. 6, pp. 5–61. The Senate was so impressed with Bentham's *Defense of Usury* (1787), that it ordered it printed as a public document. This document, also, contains the letter of Adam Smith to Bentham defending usury laws. There was, in this period, a well-marked movement to repeal all usury laws. By a series of laws (1833–54), England repealed all laws restricting the interest rate, except on mortgages, and the *Bankers' Magazine* commended these laws saying: 'capital should be set free between borrower and lender.' (*Bankers' Magazine*, IX, pp. 242, 252). W. L. Marcy, Governor of New York in 1837, considered usury laws bad since 'they assumed the guardianship of private business transactions, and endeavored to regulate the judgment and control the discretion of men in relation to the management of their ordinary affairs' (New York *Senate Documents*, 1837, I, No. 1, p. 19). Scores of other quotations could be given with the same viewpoint, from the *Bankers' Magazine*, resolutions of Boards of Trade, reports of Bank Commissioners, Governors' messages; etc. William Cobbett, veteran British Radical, considered such a move as a piece with the opposition to factory regulation in England (*History of Usury*). Perhaps the best answer to the movement to repeal came, curiously enough, from the very home of Jeffersonian Democracy. The difference in bargaining power between the borrower and lender was thus expressed: 'the borrower never can be on an equal footing to bargain with the lender. The act of borrowing implies want, necessity; the act of lending implies no such necessity.... the law therefore makes the bargain for them.' Thomas Jefferson Randolph, *Sixty Years Reminiscences of the Currency of the United States* (Charlottesville, Va., May 9,

clear that he saw its passing without great regret.[1] In 1836, when the New York Legislature was debating the repeal of the Restraining Act of 1818, prohibiting private persons from doing discount and deposit business, Gallatin expressed himself as follows: 'Banking, with the single exception of issuing paper money, should be left as free as any other species of dealing...but I can't agree with those who think that the issuing of paper currency should also be left unrestrained.... Yet, it is not perceived on what grounds a distinction can justly be made by granting charters to one set of men and refusing them to another.'[2] Although not inclined to join the hue and cry about monopoly and clearly realizing the value of monopoly as a method of regulation, he did not think that the advantages outweighed the defects.[3]

The Safety-Fund System, like the Suffolk and the large State-bank systems, encountered stormy weather in the days of Jacksonian Democracy. The attack came from two different sources; i.e., the anti-monopoly and the anti-paper money advocates. As Albert Gallatin wrote, 'the opposition to the banking system was, originally...as much against paper currency, by whomsoever issued, as against the monopoly enjoyed by the banks.'[4] There had been in New York City for several years a growing element opposed to all paper money and demanding a currency of gold and silver. As early as 1829, a certain Ebenezer Ford was elected to the Assembly on a Workingman's ticket and a platform which declared: 'the greatest knaves, imposters and paupers of the

1873). Henry Clews, in *The Wall Street Point of View* (New York, 1900), pp. 11–17, argues for freedom of contract in money bargains.

[1] Henry Adams, *Life of Albert Gallatin*, p. 561. Miss Martineau in her *Journal* of September 24, 1834, reports the following conversation with Gallatin: 'Would have no United States Bank. Would have free banking as soon as practicable. Thinks Jackson all wrong about the Bank, but has changed his opinions as to its powers. It has no political powers, but prodigious commercial. If the Bank be not necessary, better avoid allowing the power.' See in *Ibid.*, pp. 665–66, his letter to John M. Boots, June 14, 1841, in which he writes that the cause of the Bank is not one to die for.

[2] Adams, *Writings*, III, pp. 511–13. Gallatin to Frederick Beasly, New York, September 3, 1836.

[3] *Ibid.*, pp. 429–30; 'Suggestions on Banking and Currency' (1841).

[4] *Ibid.*, p. 430.

age are our bankers, who swear they have promised to pay their creditors thirty or thirty-five millions of dollars on demand, at the same time that they have, as they also swear, only three or four millions to do it with...that more than one hundred broken banks, within a few years past admonish the community to destroy banks altogether.'[1] This party, later known as the Loco-Foco party, was particularly strong among the new working class of New York City. On October 29, 1835, it captured Tammany Hall from the regular Democrats, and by the light of loco-foco matches (whence its name) adopted a series of resolutions. These, among other things, declared opposition 'to all bank charters...because we believe them founded on and as giving an impulse to principles of speculation and gambling, at war with good morals and just and equal government, and calculated to build up and strengthen in our country the odious distinction of wealth and power, against want and equal rights....'[2] Moreover, they accepted the idea that all paper money was a swindle, a view for which William Cobbett was being laughed at in the British House of Commons,[3] for which Benton was to be known as 'Old Bullion,' and which was to

[1] A. M. Simmons, *Social Forces in American History* (New York, 1918), p. 184; text of the platform. This platform, however, contained many points besides the bank clause, and like Chartism and Populism generated *ideas*, which later became the basis of constructive action. This opposition to credit money which was later to find its way into many western constitutions of the forties, was itself not new in 1829. William Cobbett had been expounding it since 1812, Jefferson had declared paper money as dangerous as standing armies, and John Adams had declared paper not backed by equal coin was a cheat on somebody. H. E. Miller, *State Banking Theories before 1860* (1928). In 1820, Jefferson had declared: 'I should say put down all banks, admit none but a *metallic circulation*....' Paul Leicester Ford, *Writings of Thomas Jefferson*, X, p. 162; Jefferson to Charles Pinckney, September 30, 1820.

[2] F. Byrdsall, *History of the Loco-Foco or Equal Rights Party* (New York, 1842). This little book is about the only source on one of the most interesting phases of American social history. It was written by the Recording-Secretary of the party during its brief existence, and a robust disciple of its ideas. His view, as he says, was that the Loco-Foco movement provided the necessary ferment or 'Methodist revival' for the Democratic party.

[3] Carlton J. H. Hayes, *Political and Social History of Modern Europe* (2 vols. New York, 1926), II, p. 110.

become general in the Mississippi Valley after the panic of 1837.

In addition to being assailed by those who wanted no banks, the Safety-Fund System was under the suspicion of those who wanted more. This demand in New York came largely from the newer areas opened up by the Erie Canal. The 'Jacksonian Migration,' which was driving the frontier into Florida, Iowa, and Texas, was also affecting western New York — an area which, in a social and economic sense, was more a part of Michigan than New York. This section wanted more banks, just as it wanted more canals. Since they could only be granted by special acts, and but a small percentage of applications could be considered, dissatisfaction grew into scandal and investigations. To relieve the pressure a law was passed requiring that all stock in new banks be sold at public auction, after three weeks' notice and with a definite limit on the amount sold to any one person. In 1836, some ninety-three applications for new bank charters were made, but only twelve were granted. In the ten counties of western New York, there was on January 1, 1836, $1,750,000 of bank capital. During the year 1836, these counties applied for $6,600,000 of capital but received $800,000.[1]

From Onondaga County, early in 1837, a petition was sent in for a general bank law, with the statement 'that moneyed corporations with special and exclusive privileges' were as un-republican as titles of nobility.[2] A petition from Alleghany County, declared that this 'new and until recently almost unknown section of the State,' had been neglected in both bank capital and internal improvement. A certain William T. Howell, 'arch pilot of loco-focoism from New York,' who had sent down a remonstrance against bank charters, did not represent this section, and the petition condemns 'bank minions,... whose illiberal souls, glutted with a profusion of banking facilities,' prevent extension to other sections.[3] In January 1837, the restraining law of 1818

[1] Chaddock, pp. 275-94. The author has a map, showing the bank capital applied for and granted.

[2] *Senate Documents*, 1837, I, No. 10, January 18, 1837.

[3] *Assembly Documents*, 1837, III, No. 200, pp. 1-13, February 17, 1837.

was repealed, thereby throwing banking open to private persons dealing in deposit and discount. This followed Gallatin's suggestion.[1] The next question was whether the Safety-Fund System should be thrown open to all without special acts.

A Senate Committee, reporting in February, complained of the great opposition to the banks and the cry that, 'the people have killed the big monster and now they must kill the little ones.' It seemed that a new code of ethics and a new category of crime had been adopted — that to be a bank official was criminal and a disqualification for public office. Moreover, thought the Committee, the cry of monopoly was largely imagination, for any man who wished could buy shares of a safety-fund bank and share its profits.[2] A Committee of the Assembly, however, took the Loco-Foco view that, 'it is a palpable fraud in bankers to pretend that they are democrats, or that any man is a democrat, who contends for bank paper. So, also, is any man anti-Jackson, who contends for bank paper, as the farewell address of that venerable patriot proves undeniably.' [3] Thus had Jackson's tilt with Nicholas Biddle fertilized the growing suspicion.

THE FREE–BANK SYSTEM

No general bank law, however, passed in 1837. It was not until 1838, almost a year after the panic of 1837, that any such law reached the statute books. Whatever effect the panic may have had in bringing about final enactment, it is clear that the driving power lay in the social and economic forces prior to the panic. This is all the clearer when it is recalled that, at least two months before the panic, the anti-monopoly forces of Michigan forced through a general bank law, March 15, 1837. Governor Marcy in his message, January 2, 1838, advised a law 'to open the business of banking to a full and free competition,' under the restriction of a general law, and a specie reserve.[4] The general law, following this recommendation, passed the Assembly on April 5, 1838,

[1] Chaddock, p. 373.
[2] *Senate Documents*, 1838, I, No. 38, pp. 1–4, February 25, 1837.
[3] *Assembly Documents*, 1837, IV, No. 302, p. 25.
[4] *Assembly Journal*, 1838, pp. 13–19.

by a vote of 86–29; [1] the Senate shortly thereafter, by a vote
of 20–8; [2] and was approved by Governor Marcy on April
18.[3]   Governor Seward, in his message of January 1, 1839,
highly commended the new system.[4] This was the famous
free-bank or general bank law of New York, which became
the model for other States and the National Bank Act.
Wherever the idea may have originated in theory, or who
was primarily responsible for its passage,[5] there can be no
doubt of its future influence.

Under the law of April 18, 1838, the issue of all notes was

---

[1] *Assembly Journal*, p. 877.   [2] *Senate Journal*, 1838, p. 480.

[3] *Assembly Journal*, 1838, p. 1140.

[4] *Senate Documents*, 1838, No. 1, p. 14.

[5] The origin of the free-bank principle of note issue, and the problem of
what men were primarily responsible for the law of 1838 are nice points
which lend themselves to historical solution little better than the origins
of the National Bank Act. The Bank Commissioners of Massachusetts
in 1865 said it was actively discussed in England following the crisis of
1825, being proposed by such writers as Ricardo and McCulloch, and
by Samuel Lloyd Jones in 1837 (see footnote 6, pp. 33–34). The idea,
however, seems to have been in the mind of an anonymous writer in the
Analectic Magazine, VI (1815), pp. 489–518, in an article signed 'W' and
entitled, 'The History of a Little Frenchman and his Bank Notes.'
H. E. Miller, in *Banking Theories in the United States before 1860*, credits
Professor John McVickar with the suggestion in a pamphlet: *Hints on
Currency and Banking* (1827). Eleazar Lord claims to have suggested the
idea of the law in *Credit, Currency and Banking* (1829 and 1834) — for
citations to pamphlets by Lord making this claim, see Chapter VI.
The National Intelligencer, January 18, 1862, during the discussions of
the National Banking System said that Lord was 'the first to propose the
plan of free banking adopted in the State of New York....' Silas M.
Stilwell claimed to have been the parent of this act as well as the National law, but his claim is discredited by the existence of a pamphlet of
his published in 1838, proposing a sort of Loan Bank (see Chapter VI
for citations to Stilwell). Eleazar Lord, in addition to claiming to have
suggested the idea in 1829, refers to a certain Isaac Bronson of New
York as being active in securing passage of the law. Bronson may have
been active for there is a pamphlet of his dated August, 1837, in which he
urges upon the Secretary the adoption of the bond security feature for a
National Bank: *Letters addressed to Levi Woodbury*. Dixon Ryan Fox in
'Decline of Aristocracy in the Politics of New York,' Columbia University *Studies*, LXXXVI, p. 403, attributes the bill to Willis Hall, Whig
of New York City. Condy Raguet was disposed to think the idea came
from Maryland, where C. F. Mayer of Baltimore had presented a bill in
1831. *Financial Register*, II, pp. 398–400.

centralized in the hands of a Comptroller of the Currency at Albany; and persons, or associations of persons, complying with the regulations, were permitted to organize banks. Whenever such a bank deposited with the Comptroller five per cent bonds of the United States, New York, or other States approved by the Comptroller, it received an equal amount of notes, stamped 'secured by the pledge of public stock.' In addition, real estate six per cent mortgages on 'improved, productive, unincumbered land' in New York, worth twice the amount of the mortgage, might be deposited as a basis of security for a maximum of fifty per cent of the total notes issued. Every note under $1000 was payable on demand at the counter of the issuing bank. If a bank failed to redeem on demand, it was liable to the noteholder for a fourteen per cent annual interest charge on the face of the suspended bill. Furthermore, the noteholder could protest non-payment before a notary public and file the protest with the Comptroller. The Comptroller was thereupon to order payment, and if after ten days payment was still refused, he was to give public notice that the notes of such bank would be redeemed by a public auction of the securities deposited. As a further protection, a twelve and a half per cent specie reserve against circulation was required to be held in the vaults of each bank. Shareholders were not individually liable, nor was there any pledge of State faith. To summarize: the noteholder was protected by an annual interest charge of fourteen per cent on suspended bills, by public securities of a par value equal to the notes issued, deposited in trust with the Comptroller and devoted exclusively to note redemption, and by a twelve and a half per cent specie reserve.[1]

Since the value of paper money is determined by the certainty or uncertainty of payment at par on demand, it will be seen that this system provided a large measure of protection. This, however, as experience proved, was insufficient to maintain parity. Certain defects were made clear by

[1] *Laws*, 1838, chap. 260; the text of this law will be found in J. R. McCulloch, *Dictionary of Commerce and Navigation* (2 vols., Philadelphia, 1852), I, pp. 150–53. An analysis of the provisions is contained in the annual report of the Comptroller, 1838, 25th Cong., 3d Sess., *House Ex. Doc.* No. 227, pp. 201 ff.

experience and remedied. The permission to use bonds of other States proved a serious defect in the forties, on account of the repudiation movement in some States. Furthermore, the principle of counter redemption forced country bank notes, current in New York City, to a discount. On May 14, 1840, these two defects were remedied by requiring that banks outside the cities of New York, Brooklyn, and Albany must maintain redemption agencies in New York City or Albany, where a maximum discount of one half per cent would be allowed; and that all future bonds deposited as a basis for the circulation of notes must be those of New York. The system, however, was weakened by the repeal of the twelve and a half specie reserve.[1] Other defects developed. Real estate mortgages as a basis for the circulation of paper money were defective, not in ultimate sufficiency but in immediate availability on forced sales.[2] Furthermore, five per cent bonds did not remain at par. By a law of April 12, 1848, these defects were remedied by increasing the quality of securities. Thereafter, New York bonds must be six per cent in place of the original five per cent, and real estate mortgages must be seven per cent taken at forty per cent of the value of land, in place of the original six per cent taken at fifty per cent of the value of the land. Fillmore in his famous report advised that mortgages be abandoned entirely, and the use of high quality United States and States stocks be substituted. He predicted that if all States would adopt the free-bank system and use Government bonds as security, it would lead to a National System and avoid the use of a National Bank — a prediction realized fifteen years later.[3] This progressive restriction of the note issue basis encountered a difficulty. New York State was rapidly retiring its public debt which

---

[1] *Laws*, 1840, chap. 363. 31st Cong., 1st Sess., *House Ex. Doc.* No. 68, pp. 133–46, a brilliant survey of the first decade of the free-bank system by Millard Fillmore, in December, 1848, after his election to the Vice-Presidency. The county bankers of New York, irked by this requirement, started a fight for their own agencies, similar to the Boston Bank of Mutual Redemption. Not until 1858 did it successfully get under way. *Bankers' Magazine*, X, pp. 54, 140, 244, 306, 570; XII, pp. 424, 631, 838, 919.

[2] 34th Cong., 1st Sess., *House Ex. Doc.* No. 102, p. 124.

[3] Buffalo Historical Society *Publications*, X, pp. 276–83.

produced a restriction on the volume of currency at the very moment when the business cycle was swinging upward in the fifties. This inelasticity, which was characteristic also of the National System, was inherent in a note issue founded on the public debt. New York partially met the difficulty in a law of April 10, 1849, by allowing the use of United States six per cent bonds for a maximum of fifty per cent of the deposited security.[1] In the mean time the constitution of 1846 had provided additional security. The billholder had been given priority in the general assets of an insolvent bank, and it was further provided that, on January 1, 1850, stockholders should be individually liable for 'all debts and liabilities of every kind.' The constitution furthermore definitely committed the State to the principle of general incorporation.[2]

The experience of this system developed some interesting facts. Between 1840 and 1850, some thirty-two banks suspended payment, with a circulation of $1,468,245, and when all the protection for notes was exhausted, billholders lost $325,487. This amounted to about one half per cent loss per annum on the total circulation of the system. From 1850 to 1861, twenty-seven banks failed, with a circulation of $1,648,000 and a loss to billholders of $72,849, an average annual loss of only $4,800 on a $22,000,000 circulation for the entire free-bank system. After 1861 there were no suspensions. The experience for the entire history of the system showed an average annual loss of about one tenth per cent. In regard to particular types of securities Fillmore reported in 1848 that mortgages yielded 67.71 per cent, and New York five per cent bonds yielded 92.86 per cent. These figures, of course, gradually rose towards par as the basis of security was strengthened in the last decade of the system.[3]

By the time the National System was adopted the New

[1] *Bankers' Magazine*, July–December, 1849, pp. 25–35, text of the new laws of 1849. This was further extended in 1863 allowing United States stock to the extent of two thirds of the total.

[2] *Senate Doc.*, 1849, II, No. 42, pp. 1–6.

[3] Louis Carroll Root, 'New York Bank Currency,' in *Sound Currency*, II. The author was an assistant to the Indianapolis Monetary Commission (1897–98); secretary of the Sound Currency Committee of Reform (1895–1906); vice-president of a New York City bank; and recently connected with a New Orleans bank.

York free-bank system had evolved into one of the soundest of the Nation, on a par with those developed at New Orleans and Boston in the same period. Its provisions for note redemption were operating with reasonable effectiveness. Freedom of incorporation, individual liability, priority of billholder, a high class of securities as a basis for circulation, and par redemption in the commercial centers of the State were the main features. Yet it still had some defects. Some of these were inherent in a circulation based on public securities, others were capable of legislative remedy. The lack of any provision of reserves for circulation and deposits, such as had been adopted in New Orleans, was perhaps the most serious defect. Inelasticity was incorporated into the National System along with the virtues of the free-bank system, and became a problem for the future.

THE NEW YORK CLEARING HOUSE

Another feature of the New York bank system, not particularly a part of the standard free-bank principle, was the clearing house. Originally suggested by Gallatin in 1831, the idea waited over twenty years for practical application. On August 23, 1853, the representatives of thirty-eight New York City banks in session at the Merchants Bank appointed a committee to prepare a plan. At a meeting, September 13, a plan was adopted to begin operation on October 11, in the basement of Number 14 in Wall Street. A manager was to be appointed whose duty it was to prepare statements of balances due from member banks. Settling clerks representing the various banks were to assemble at nine o'clock each morning and the balances were to be struck by 1 P.M. George D. Lyman, second teller of Hamilton's old Bank of North America, was elected manager and served until 1864. One of the unexpected results of these daily balances was a healthy curtailment of loans, amounting to something like $14,000,000 in the first three months of its operation; a result which stabilized the money market of 1854.[1] The total

[1] *Bankers' Magazine*, VII, p. 920; VIII, pp. 344, 445, 579; IX, pp. 409–13, text of constitution of the clearing house drafted by George Curtis, June 6, 1854, which has remained in force with some amendments since its adoption. J. S. Gibbons, *The Banks of New York, Their Dealers, The*

of clearings for the first year of its operation was $5,886,753,-
538; with only $304,152,457 specie exchange.[1] For the first
five years of its operation October, 1853, to October, 1858,
with total clearings of over thirty-one billions, only about
four and one half per cent specie exchange was necessary for
the forty-nine banks affiliated.[2] In the money stringency of
1860, as also in 1873, 1884, and 1907, the New York clearing house, by a purely voluntary effort, undertook to provide
the much-needed elasticity of credit by issuing temporary
clearing house certificates. The principle used was somewhat similar to that legalized in the functioning of the
Federal Reserve System, members of the clearing house de-
positing their securities with the clearing house which issued
certificates in exchange, the member banks mutually agree-
ing to accept them in payment of balances. By so doing the
tightening of the market was eased at a period when the
most serious defect of an inelastic credit and currency system
manifested itself.[3]

Between 1853 and 1865 clearing houses were established
in some seven cities: Boston, 1855; Philadelphia, Baltimore,
and Cleveland, 1856; Worcester, 1861; Chicago and Pitts-
burgh, 1865.[4] At Philadelphia with nineteen member banks,
its experience for the first year of operation required about
six per cent specie balance after clearings.[5]

MICHIGAN WILDCATS

The history of the New York free-bank law proved that
the principle, under proper safeguards, could evolve into a
sound system; the Michigan free-bank law, on the contrary,
demonstrated that, lacking proper safeguards, it could degenerate into irresponsible 'wildcatting.' Michigan, in the
thirties, was in a process of tumultuous development, as set-

Clearing House, and the Panic of 1857 (New York, 1858), pp. 292–342,
a discussion of the clearing house and its constitution. James Graham
Cannon, "Clearing Houses," in National Monetary Commission *Reports*
(Washington, 1908), chaps. XIII–XIV, early history and daily routine.

[1] *Bankers' Magazine*, IX, p. 413.   [2] *Ibid.*, XIII, p. 882.
[3] W. A. Scott, *Money and Banking* (New York, 1926), p. 187.
[4] *Bankers' Magazine*, XXXII, p. 343.
[5] *Ibid.*, XII, p. 680; XIII, p. 663.

tlers pressed to the lake shore over the Erie Canal. These emigrants had the anti-monopoly antecedents of the western counties of New York, from which many of them came, as well as the itch for banks and internal improvements. Early banking in Michigan, therefore, became involved in the speculative forces of the day, particularly land speculation. Out of these circumstances grew the 'wildcat banks,' their collapse in the panic, and the distress of the forties.

By the close of 1836, sixteen charters had been granted to banks by the Territory and State.[1] Some of these were operating under a law of March 28, 1836, providing for a Bank Commissioner and a safety-fund of the New York type.[2] These charters, however, failed to satisfy the Michigan appetite, and on March 15, 1837, the so-called 'killer of monopolies' was passed with small opposition.[3] This was the parent of a numerous progeny of 'wildcats.'

By this law the business of banking was thrown open to 'any person or persons resident in the State...desirous of establishing a bank.' Notes were to be protected by a safety-fund, by certain types of collateral securities, and by both directors' and stockholders' individual liability. The safety-fund was to be accumulated and applied as in New York; securities were to consist either of real estate mortgages taken at 'true cash value,' or personal notes 'executed by resident freeholders'; a director was 'liable to the extent of his individual property, and stockholders to the amount of stock held'; thirty per cent of the capital must be paid in before beginning business; and a board of three Commissioners was to supervise.[4] It would appear at first sight that this law was a most restrictive one, but examined more closely, the restrictions disappear. Less than one third of the capital must be paid in before issuing notes on the total capital; the safety-fund did not accumulate fast enough to redeem notes

[1] *First Annual Report of the Bank Commissioner*, January 5, 1837, in 25th Cong., 3d Sess., *House Ex. Doc.* No. 227, pp. 802–12.

[2] *Michigan Laws* (1835–36), pp. 157–65.

[3] Floyd Benjamin Streeter, *Political Parties in Michigan*, p. 33, gives the House vote as 39–4, and the Senate vote as 14–1.

[4] *Report of the Bank Commissioner*, December 6, 1837, in 25th Cong., 2d Sess., *Senate Doc.* No. 471, p. 458.

of banks failing in the panic; and the very strong liability features were rendered ineffective by court decisions.[1] Moreover, ingenious methods were devised for evading inspection, and, indeed, for evading the requirement of thirty per cent paid-in capital. The fundamental defect, however, was the type of securities permitted. Real estate mortgages were bad enough, especially when taken at 'true cash value' assessed by sympathetic county officials in a period of inflated land values and speculative optimism. This value placed on undiscovered 'farms' or remote 'city-lots' in the woods, might be fifty times the actual value after the panic. But, in addition the law permitted a circulation based on personal notes of 'resident freeholders.' Before the close of 1838 nearly fifty banks were organized under this law, and the result was a collapse equal to that of the land banks of the cotton South.[2]

When the Commissioners inspected a certain Jackson County Bank in 1838, they reported as follows: 'Beneath the counter nine boxes were pointed out by the teller as containing $1000 each. The teller selected one of these boxes and opened it; this was examined and appeared to be full of American half dollars. One of the Commissioners then selected a box which he opened and found the same to consist of a superficies only of silver, while the remaining portions consisted of lead and ten-penny nails. The Commissioners then proceeded to open the remaining silver boxes; they presented the same contents precisely, with the single exception in which the substratum was window glass broken into small pieces.'[3] Other banks inspected showed similar evasions,

[1] Thomas M. Cooley, 'State Bank Issues in Michigan,' in Michigan Political Science Society *Publications*, I (1893), p. 14. The author was a prominent member of the Michigan bar, and first chairman of the Interstate Commerce Commission.

[2] 25th Cong., 3d Sess., *House Ex. Doc.* No. 227, pp. 640–42.

[3] 26th Cong., 1st Sess., *House Ex. Doc.* No. 172, p. 1109. One of the Commissioners was Alpheus Felch, later Governor and United States Senator from Michigan. He was one of the four voting against the law in the House in 1837. One writer describes conditions in a 'wild-cat' town as follows: 'A trip in the fall of 1838 on horseback discovered the palaces of "rag barons" to consist of a very small hotel, a store, and a bank building costing $1,711. There were also included in the category

some presenting 'specie certificates' supposed to represent specie deposited elsewhere. As the Commissioners passed about the State on inspection they discovered other ingenious evasions such as specie hurriedly transferred from place to place as inspection threatened and banks established in remote places inaccessible for inspection or note redemption. The Commissioners in 1839 related their adventures as follows: 'The singular spectacle was presented of officers of the State seeking for banks in situations the most remote from trade, and finding at every step an increase of labor by the discovery of new and unknown organizations.... Gold and silver flew about the country with the celerity of magic, its sounds were heard in the depths of the forest, yet like the wind one knew not whence it came, nor whither it was going. Such were a few of the difficulties against which the commissioners had to contend. The vigilance of a regiment of them would scarcely have been adequate against a host of bank emissaries, who scoured the country to anticipate their coming and the indefatigable spies who hung upon their path....' They estimated that over $1,000,000 of this wildcat currency had been placed in circulation.[1]

hundreds of city lots for sale in currency of any kind.... At this date the city lots are not sold, and but for its banking history, the city would be unknown.' T. H. Hinchman, *Banks and Banking in Michigan* (Detroit, 1887), pp. 39–40.

[1] 25th Cong., 3d Sess., *House Ex. Doc.* No. 227, pp. 641–42, January 18, 1839. Alpheus Felch, one of the Commissioners, described the situation to A. D. White as follows: 'He said that he and a brother examiner made an excursion through the state in a sleigh with a pair of good horses in order to inspect the various banks established in remote villages and hamlets.... After visiting a few of these and finding that each had the amount of specie required by law, the examiners began to note a curious similarity between the specie packages in the different banks, and before long their attention was attracted to another curious fact, which was that wherever they went, they were preceded by a sleigh drawn by especially fleet horses. On making careful examination, they found that the sleigh bore from bank to bank a number of kegs of specie sufficient to enable each bank in its turn to show the examiners a temporary basis of hard money for its output of paper.' *Autobiography of A. D. White* (2 vols., New York, 1917), I, pp. 184–85. Other picturesque accounts are: H. M. Utley, 'Wild Cat Banking System of Michigan,' in *Michigan Pioneer Collections*, V, pp. 209–22; T. H. Hinchman, *Banks and Banking in Michigan* (Detroit, 1887); and Alpheus Felch,

By the close of 1839 only four of these banks were operating, and these soon expired.[1] The law of 1837 was repealed by an act of April 16, 1839, entitled: 'An act to more effectually protect the public against various frauds,'[2] leaving thousands of dollars of Michigan currency, artistically engraved by Rawdon, Wright and Hatch, to mold in old garrets and adorn the walls of pioneer cabins. After an unsuccessful effort to organize a bank on the model of the Indiana State Bank,[3] enthusiasm cooled and few banks were created prior to the Civil War. By December, 1861, only four small institutions existed in the State with a total circulation of $120,124.[4]

THE SUFFOLK SYSTEM

The Suffolk System of Boston was the most important system of New England before the National Bank Act. Boston, as the commercial center of New England, very naturally attracted to her counters the bank notes of a wide area, and the circulation of so much 'foreign paper' created a serious problem. Much of it had been issued by country banks in remote parts of Vermont, Maine, and New Hampshire; and was ordinarily at a discount (at times as high as six per cent), varying with the distance from Boston and the credit of the issuing bank. Before the Suffolk System was introduced, the methods of redemption were crude and inefficient. A collector, dispatched by individual Boston banks or representing a group of them, would go with the collected notes of New England banks, present them for redemption at their counters and take the specie kegs back to Boston.[5] The defects of this method are clear and it was from these circumstances that the new system originated.

'Early Banks and Banking in Michigan,' in *Michigan Pioneer Collections*, II (1880), pp. 111–26.

[1] 26th Cong., 1st Sess., *House Ex. Doc.* No. 172, p. 1294.

[2] *Michigan Laws* (1839), p. 121.

[3] *Ibid.*, pp. 37–64, April 2, 1839.

[4] 37th Cong., 1st Sess., *House Ex. Doc.* No. 25, p. 172. Those operating were: Michigan Insurance Company, Peninsular Bank, Farmers and Mechanics with a branch at Niles, and the Michigan State Bank.

[5] Everett Birney Stackpole, 'State Banking in Maine,' in *Sound Currency*, VII, No. 5, p. 71.

The famous Suffolk Bank, which became the center of the new system, began operations on State Street, April 1, 1818.[1] In 1819 it collected large quantities of country paper, and presented them at the counters of country banks for redemption. This caused an outcry and the Suffolk proposed redemption at its counters in Boston, if the country banks would keep a permanent deposit of $5000 in its vaults. This proposal was not accepted at the time, but the practice followed after 1825 was based on this principle. In the mean time, the Suffolk continued its policy of collecting foreign paper at a discount in Boston and sending it in large amounts to the issuing banks. In 1821 an agent was dispatched to a bank in Maine with $3000 for redemption. The cashier, unable to meet this sudden demand, first offered notes of Boston banks, and when this was refused, sought refuge in cunning. He began to count out the specie but counted so slowly that he delivered but $500 in one day. The Suffolk agent thereupon left and the Maine bank was sued for the two per cent monthly penalty prescribed by law on the notes of suspended banks. The case was decided in favor of the Suffolk.[2]

The system was placed in effective operation in 1825 by the coöperation of the Suffolk and the important Boston banks. With a common fund of $300,000, they proceeded to buy large amounts of country paper and demand specie redemption. With this weapon, capable of causing suspension for the majority of country banks, this so-called 'Holy Alliance' forced the adoption of its plan. Each country bank was required to keep a permanent deposit of $2000 on each $100,000 of capital, and a redemption balance in addition. Country notes were cleared daily.[3]

[1] David Rice Whitney, *The Suffolk Bank* (Boston, 1878), p. 3. General discussions of New England banking will be found in: L. Carroll Root, 'Twenty Years of Bank Currency Based on General Commercial Assets,' *Sound Currency*, VIII, pp. 209–32; and L. Carroll Root, 'New England Bank Currency,' *Sound Currency*, II, pp. 2–32. A. R. Hasse, *Index of Economic Material in Documents of the States of the United States, Massachusetts* (Washington, 1908), is the best guide.

[2] James D. Magee, 'The Fight Against Par Check Redemption,' in *Journal of Political Economy*, XXXI (1923), pp. 433–45.

[3] *Bankers' Magazine*, VII, p. 337. It is necessary to note that this was not a system of clearings for checks on deposits such as developed in New York thirty years later.

The method by which this system operated was described by a contemporary Boston financier as follows: 'Certain banks in Boston have contributed a sum agreed on, to a common fund, and in consideration of the use of that fund, one of them, the Suffolk, undertakes to receive all bills of New England banks as cash, and collect them from the country banks. The country banks are invited to keep a sum in deposit at the Suffolk Bank for redemption of these bills. If they decline, the bills are sent home for payment, in which case, nothing but a legal payment in coin will be received.' [1]

This method was naturally unpopular with country banks, due to what they were disposed to regard as coercive methods and undue centralization of credit at Boston. The reaction of the country banks in general may be inferred from the fight between the new system and a Worcester bank in 1827. Failing to accept the Suffolk invitation to maintain a permanent deposit, the cashier of the Worcester bank suddenly found himself confronted by a Suffolk agent demanding specie for $48,000 in notes. The cashier was able to redeem only $28,000 on that day but called at the Suffolk counter the following day with the remainder. This delayed redemption was refused, however, and upon suit in the courts the Suffolk collected the two per cent penalty on suspended bills.[2] A petition to the legislature of Maine in 1837 complained of the necessity of laying down 'bags of *Tribute Money at the Feet of the President of the Suffolk Bank*,' and a majority committee report favored a bill forbidding redemption outside of the State.[3] The Bank Commissioners of Maine, however, in 1838 reported that the system was sound and mutually beneficial. In 1841 they declared: 'Our banks have accomplished their great object of furnishing a sound currency... in consequence of its redemption at par in the great central market of the country.' Banks which refused to enter the system found their bills at discounts in Boston

[1] Nathan Appleton, *Remarks on Currency and Banking* (Boston, 1841), p. 10.

[2] Magee, 'Fight Against Par Check Redemption.'

[3] Stackpole, 'State Banking in Maine,' pp. 73–76. A Maine writer expresses his opposition in *Hunt's Merchants' Magazine*, XXVI (1851), pp. 316–23; 439–47.

and Portland, while the notes of member banks circulated at par over New England.[1]

Elsewhere in New England the system operated with equal effectiveness. The president of a Vermont bank declared that his notes 'went to Boston as if drawn by a magnet,' his entire circulation being cleared every thirty days.[2] In Connecticut, where the circulation was cleared at Boston every sixty days, the State authorities commended the system for exerting a restraining influence on circulation.[3] Vermont placed a one per cent tax on the notes of any bank failing to redeem in Boston; and in 1851 it was estimated that two hundred and fifty times as much Vermont currency was redeemed in Boston as over the counters. The total annual clearings at Boston was estimated at $244,000,-000 in 1851,[4] and in 1855 at $350,000,000.[5] According to the figures of the Suffolk Bank, a very marked contraction of country notes was forced during the first year of the new system. In 1822, the circulation of Massachusetts banks more than fifty miles distant from Boston was one hundred and thirty-one per cent of capital, but in 1826 it had been reduced to sixty-four per cent. The circulation of New Hampshire banks more than fifty miles from Portsmouth was one hundred and sixty-five per cent in 1818; and in 1826 it was seventy per cent. Country banks of Maine contracted circulation from one hundred and ten per cent to forty-eight per cent.[6] Another important result noted was the smaller specie reserve needed by member banks. Vermont authorities in 1853 declared that banks needed from twenty to twenty-five per cent reserves if they remained outside, but about five per cent as member banks.[7]

Opposition to this control of circulation had long been felt by country banks, but it was not until after the panic of

[1] Stackpole, pp. 57; 73–76.

[2] L. E. Chittenden, *Personal Reminiscences* (New York, 1893), pp. 26–27.

[3] 31st Cong., 1st Sess., *House Ex. Doc.* No. 68, pp. 90–91.

[4] 32d Cong., 2d Sess., *House Ex. Doc.* No. 66, pp. 31–32.

[5] *Bankers' Magazine*, X, p. 697.

[6] *Remarks on the Currency of the New England States* (Boston, 1826).

[7] *Bankers' Magazine*, VII, p. 506.

1857 that an organized movement succeeded in breaking it. The movement of the country banks to organize their own redemption agency in Boston took form as early as 1853, when a bill chartering such an agency was rejected by the legislature.[1] The Bank of Mutual Redemption was chartered May 21, 1855.[2] The original charter required a capital of $1,000,000, and the difficulty of subscribing this amount delayed its organization. On May 20, 1857, its minimum capital was reduced to $500,000, which was subscribed and the new agency went into operation August 2, 1858.[3] The Bank of Mutual Redemption, however, became involved at once in a warm controversy with the Suffolk, which refused to present its collected notes at the counter of the new agency, but insisted on sending them home to the individual banks. A convention of country banks decided on withdrawing their deposits from the Suffolk by October 10, 1858, while Suffolk attorneys prepared learned briefs on the legal right to demand redemption from individual banks. The Boston banks generally supported the Suffolk in its fight, but the latter finally surrendered with the curt statement that 'the business of assorting country paper will not be continued by this bank after 30th November, 1858.'[4]

The Bank of Mutual Redemption did not destroy the Suffolk System. It merely transferred part of the business to a new redemption agency. As the Bank Commissioners of Maine observed in 1861, the question as to whether the country banks redeemed their own paper in Boston or the Suffolk did it for them was less important than that '*the thing be done.*'[5]

Two other points remain to be noted respecting Massachusetts banking. In 1851 a general free-bank law was enacted of the New York type, although few banks organized under this system.[6] More important is the fact that Samuel

[1] *Bankers' Magazine*, VIII, p. 92.

[2] 34th Cong., 3d Sess., *House Ex. Doc.* No. 87, pp. 67–68.

[3] *Bankers' Magazine*, XII, p. 70.

[4] *Ibid.*, XIII, pp. 384 ff.; documents relating to fight in September and October, 1858.

[5] 37th Cong., 3d Sess., *House Ex. Doc.* No. 25, p. 5.

[6] Massachusetts *Public Documents* (1865), III, pp. 38–56, gives a

Hooper as a member of the Legislature in 1858 was largely instrumental in securing the enactment of the fifteen per cent reserve law of 1858, and that he was already conscious of the necessity of national action in currency regulation. It was by this route that the Louisiana reserve principle reached the National Bank Act.

BANK OF THE STATE OF SOUTH CAROLINA

By 1837, banking in South Carolina was centralized, almost exclusively, in the city of Charleston. Outside the city there existed two small independent organizations, at Columbia and Cheraw; and a few branches and collection agencies operated by the Charleston banks. Economic life in South Carolina centered about the port of Charleston, and it was here that six of the largest and oldest banks in the State were located.[1] Although ten of the thirteen new organizations created between 1837–1860 were outside Charleston; yet the centralization was still evident.[2] Only one of these Charleston banks will be considered.

The Bank of the State of South Carolina was entirely owned by the State and acted as its fiscal agent. The directors could issue 'such sums as they deemed expedient and safe,' its total debts were limited to two hundred per cent of its capital, and it was backed by the faith and credit of the State. Its charter contained little that could be regarded as advanced banking principles. Its success, therefore, must

brief sketch of banking in the State since colonial times. Concerning the free-bank principle it says: 'The principle is not a new one. As early as 1825–26... it was earnestly advocated in England by many of her leading statesmen, and by such writers as Ricardo and McCulloch. In 1837... Samuel Lloyd Jones, in various papers of great ability, urged the separation of the issue from the bank department of the Bank of England.'

[1] 24th Cong., 1st Sess., *House Ex. Doc.* No. 65, pp. 138–40. The following were the six Charleston banks with their capitalization, branches, and dates of organization: Bank of South Carolina (1802), $1,000,000; State Bank of South Carolina (1802), $1,000,000; Union Bank (1810), $1,000,000; Planters' and Mechanics' Bank (1810), $1,000,000 with collection agencies at Camden and Cheraw; Bank of the State (1812), $1,000,000, branches at Camden and Columbia, collection agencies at Hamburg and Georgetown; Bank of Charleston (1834), $2,000,000.

[2] 36th Cong., 2d Sess., *House Ex. Doc.* No. 77, pp. 194–95; 200–03.

be primarily regarded as due to the conservatism by which it was operated, rather than to the positive restrictions of law.[1] Before the panic it held a twenty per cent reserve and Judge Colcock, President since 1830, announced a very successful year, but gave significant warning against the future. He noted a great demand for specie in America, drawing from Europe to such an extent that he feared the Bank of England would take steps to prevent further specie export.[2] In fact the Bank of England had already taken measures to strengthen its reserves and there can be no doubt of the effect of this action on the volume of American specie.[3]

In company with the Chemical Bank of New York, the State Bank of Indiana, and the State Bank of Missouri, the Bank of the State of South Carolina did not suspend specie payments in 1837, nor did it during the second suspension of 1839.[4] Furthermore, in the midst of the depression period of 1838, a fire destroyed the principal buildings of the commercial part of Charleston,[5] and the State issued $2,000,000 in Fire Loan Bonds. These were sold principally to Baring Brothers of London, and the proceeds used by the bank to make loans for rebuilding the city.[6] Despite these facts the bank made advances to the State to meet revenue deficits, and sums were carried to the Sinking Fund to retire internal improvement bonds of 1820, due in 1840. All this was done in the face of large specie withdrawals for note redemption and a reluctant policy in pressing farmers for loan collection. Between October, 1839, and June, 1840, so great was the specie withdrawal that the bank redeemed its entire circulation.[7] What is still more remarkable is the fact that a large quantity of its loans were on agricultural paper, usually regarded as the weakest since it is long-time credit. Presi-

[1] *Acts*, 1812, pp. 127–40.

[2] 24th Cong., 2d Sess., *House Ex. Doc.* No. 65, pp. 138–40; 25th Cong., 2d Sess., *House Ex. Doc.* No. 79, p. 497.

[3] *Annual Register*, 1837, pp. 171–74. This factor has already been fully discussed in Chapter I.

[4] *Reports and Resolutions*, 1839, pp. 14–16. The Bank of Charleston continued payments during the same period.

[5] *Ibid.*, 1838, pp. 1–2.   [6] *Ibid.*, 1840, pp. 4–5; 1843, pp. 31–49.

[7] *Ibid.*, 1839, pp. 14–16; 1840, pp. 19–28; 1843, p. 43.

dent Elmore declared, however, that of the seven Charleston banks, the five which suspended had loans based on mercantile short-time paper; and declared that although mercantile credit was more brisk, agricultural credit was slower but with less risk.[1]

By 1843, the worst of the depression period had been weathered, under the able management of Franklin P. Elmore, President since 1839. The bank was faced, however, like most large banks in the forties, by considerable opposition. Governor Hammond's message of 1843 was distinctly anti-bank, and his recommendations, if adopted, would have amounted to virtual liquidation. He proposed that it be forced to retire $500,000 of State bonds every year, and pay all the interest on the State debt. Either of these requirements, President Elmore insisted, would force liquidation. If no additional burdens were added he felt sure it could gradually retire all bonds as they came due.[2] As a counter-attack against this move of the governor, Elmore, by correspondence with London firms holding the Fire Loan Bonds, with General McDuffie, who had negotiated them, and Edward Everett, American Minister at London, collected documents showing that liquidation of the bank would be regarded abroad as repudiation. General McDuffie affirmed that in negotiating the bonds he had emphasized the point that future profits of the bank would be devoted to their redemption.[3] Hambro and Son, of London, regarded closing the bank as a violation of agreement and certain to affect 'American stocks' in general. Baring Brothers felt that the prevailing distrust of 'securities of the United States' would excite general loss of credit; and Edward Everett declared that closing the bank would cause American credit to suffer, since there existed in England a 'very great sensitiveness' as to American securities. This he conceded might be only a temporary result providing security for the bonds as good as future profits was substituted. South Carolina bonds, however, did not fall in the London

[1] *Reports and Resolutions*, 1843, pp. 22–25. It must be said, however, that the reason why agricultural credit is the weakest is not the question of ultimate risk but precisely the point that it is slower in an emergency.

[2] *Ibid.*, 1843, pp. 31–49.   [3] *Ibid.*, 1843, pp. 54–55.

market. In 1843 Elmore instructed his broker in London to buy up bonds if they fell to any great extent and only a few were purchased on account of the prevailing high prices.[1] These moves together with a report of a joint committee of the Legislature in 1844 prevented liquidation.[2] Besides its other loans and political difficulties the bank in conjunction with other Charleston banks assisted the Georgia Railroad and Banking Company in its efforts to construct a road from Augusta to Atlanta, thence to connect with the Tennessee River. Railroad connections were then to be opened from Charleston to prevent a competing road from diverting the trade of that highway of the 'mighty west' to Savannah.[3]

The fight, started in 1843, was renewed with greater vigor in 1846. Numerous resolutions demanding separation of bank and State, were presented to the Legislature of 1846, but were reported unfavorably by a majority of the committee, as equivalent to a violation of faith.[4] The opposition insisted that they intended no repudiation but publicity instead of 'Bank secrecy,' and an immediate application of all bank assets to State debts.[5] The following year a special investigation to examine for 'mismanagement' reported its condition satisfactory and that it would be able to retire the State debt as it became due.[6] In 1848 the opposition was strong enough to pass a resolution in the Legislature against a recharter,[7] and the message of the Governor in 1849 recommended a ten-year liquidation period. The fall of cotton from thirteen cents to six cents per pound, on account of European revolutions, contributed to the growing attacks on the bank, and its lenient collection policy did not add to its profits but supplied an argument against it.[8] Opposition was also strong enough, in 1849, to secure a majority committee report for immediate liquidation.[9] A

---

[1] *Reports and Resolutions*, 1846, pp. 49–68, contains collected correspondence of 1843.

[2] *Ibid.*, 1844, p. 62.   [3] *Ibid.*, 1845, pp. 39–41; 47–48.

[4] *Ibid.*, 1846, pp. 41–49.   [5] *Ibid.*, 1846, pp. 69–71.

[6] *Ibid.*, 1847, pp. 58–68.   [7] *Ibid.*, 1848, p. 243.

[8] *Ibid.*, 1849, pp. 32–46.

[9] *Reports and Resolutions*, 1849, pp. 98–119. The minority report, pp. 135–39.

bill was introduced to that end by Mr. Memminger, chairman of the Ways and Means Committee of the House, and later Secretary of Treasury in the Confederacy. Memminger favored the free-bank system of New York.[1] This move to close out the bank failed, however, largely due to the influence of Franklin P. Elmore, who upon the death of Calhoun resigned the presidency of the bank, and became United States Senator. In a series of articles in the press, and by pamphlets, he successfully counteracted the anti-bank move.[2]

After 1850 there appears to have been no organized effort to liquidate the bank, but in the few years following some of the ground was cut from under it by chartering independent banks in the interior. Hitherto, banking capital had been concentrated at Charleston, and by means of its branches and agencies, the bank of the State controlled the interior business. The effect of these new charters was to reduce the profits of the bank.[3] Passing through the panic of 1857 successfully, its management had foresight enough to begin a contraction policy in 1860. From February to September, 1860, during the presidential campaign of that year, its circulation was sharply contracted.[4]

During the war, the bank continued to pay interest to London firms on the State debt, build up the sinking fund for the principal, and advance to the State. It, furthermore, made large loans to the Confederacy, particularly for the building of the Merrimac.[5] After the war, it was placed in liquidation, and banking thenceforth became national.[6]

[1] He proposed a law in December, 1857, providing for the retirement of all existing notes and the issue of a new circulation secured by bond deposits. (Pamphlet, Charleston, 1858, pp. 29–37.)

[2] Franklin Parker Elmore, *Defense of the Bank of the State of South Carolina* (Columbia, 1850).

[3] *Reports and Resolutions*, 1854, p. 81. By 1854 it had extended its interior agencies to Rome, Georgia, and St. Mary's, Sumterville, and Newberry in South Carolina.

[4] 38th Cong., 2d Sess., *House Ex. Doc.* No. 77, pp. 194–95. The success with which the cotton export centers of Charleston and New Orleans passed through the panic of 1857, no doubt intensified the myth of King Cotton.

[5] *Reports and Resolutions*, 1866, pp. 57–61.

[6] *Acts of South Carolina*, 1868–69, p. 259.

CHAPTER III
STATE BANKING IN THE OLD NORTHWEST

THE development of banking in the American West must be viewed in relation to the credit needs of that area and the cycles of its economic history. Kentucky, Tennessee, and Ohio received the major thrust of the first migration, ending about 1803 with the admission of the State of Ohio. Banking institutions in the West first appeared in this period at such commercial centers as Louisville and Cincinnati. The Kentucky Insurance Company of 1802 was primarily engaged in insuring cargoes for the New Orleans river trade, and the Miami Exporting Company was organized in 1803 to deal in river shipping. Both institutions, in the course of time, accepted deposits and issued notes. The next expansion period occurred in the decade preceding the panic of 1819. It gathered momentum in the period of embargo and war, and in the years from the peace to the panic, assumed the proportions of a 'great migration.' This 'Ohio fever' was arrested by the depression of the early twenties but not before it had added to the Union the new States of Alabama, Louisiana, Mississippi, Indiana, Illinois, and Missouri.

One of the most pressing problems of the new communities was that of credit for land and improvements. Credit for land was generously extended under the Federal land law of 1800 and the Government had shown some disposition to extend aid for internal improvements, but the States ˅re not yet ready to borrow in the money markets of Eu. ɔpe. Many ordinary business enterprises, therefore, used their own credit and issued promissory notes which circulated as paper money. An Ohio clergyman in 1814 wrote: 'During this year, a money mania like an epidemic seized the people. There were seven banking institutions established in Jefferson County, one of which is said to have been kept in a lady's chest. But it did not stop here —

merchants, tavern keepers, butchers, and bakers became bankers.'

The early twenties were a period of depression. Westward migration slackened, land sales fell sharply, despondency succeeded optimism, and banks 'cast as the hero in the first act... in the second became the detected villain.' Andrew Jackson of Tennessee, home from the wars, stormed against a proposed Loan Office and acquired a prejudice which he carried for life, like his scar of the Revolution. Henry Clay earned a reputation as a sound money man in Kentucky — a State in the throes of bitter relief legislation and furious politics. In Missouri, Moses Austin declared his bank stock 'not worth a cent' and left in disgust for Texas. Thomas Hart Benton, formerly a bank director, formed a suspicion of banks and paper money as deep as that of Andrew Jackson himself.

By the late twenties, however, another migration moved toward the region of cheap land — estimated by the Secretary of the Treasury in 1827 as requiring five hundred years to settle. Land sales quickened, canals and railroads were projected and sometimes built, and banks again assumed the rôle of hero. The central Government had stopped Federal aid for internal improvements and credit for land, and States took recourse to the surplus capital of Europe. 'The whole Mississippi Valley was filled with the noise and upheaval of the new boom period.' Before it was arrested by the panic of 1837, Arkansas and Michigan had been added to the Union, the Republic of Texas created, and the frontier thrust into Florida, Iowa, and Wisconsin. With the panic came the distress of the 'hungry forties' and the no-bank and repudiation movement of the 'prostrate West.' But there was also a tendency toward stability and reform.[1]

[1] Frederick Logan Paxson, *History of the American Frontier* (New York, 1924), pp. 190; 228; 232; 286. Charles A. Beard, *Rise of American Civilization* (2 vols., New York, 1927), II, p. 269. R. G. Thwaites, *Early Western Travels*, IX, 'Flint's Letters from America' (1818), pp. 130–36; 219–28. A. M. Stickles 'Relief Legislation and the Origin of the Court Controversy in Kentucky,' in Indiana University *Studies*, XII (1925). For Jackson's attitude on early banking in Tennessee see: New York Public Library *Bulletin*, IV (1900), pp. 189–90, and Wm. Gouge, *Curse of*

THE OHIO SYSTEM

On January 1, 1837, thirty-two banks were operating in Ohio. Five of the largest were at Cincinnati, two each at Cleveland and Columbus, and the remaining twenty-three at smaller towns in the State. The largest was the Commercial Bank of Cincinnati, which had an agency at St. Louis; and the oldest was the Miami Exporting Company, chartered in 1803 and the oldest bank in the Northwest.[1] By 1840 the total number of banks in Ohio had

Paper Money (London, 1833), p. 96. For early Kentucky banking see: E. G. Griffith, 'Early Banking in Kentucky,' in Mississippi Valley Historical Association *Proceedings*, II (1910), pp. 168–81; Basil W. Duke, *History of the Bank of Kentucky* (Louisville, 1895); and A. R. Hasse, *Index...Kentucky* (1910), pp. 62–103. Some scattering material is presented in T. P. Abernethy, 'Early Banking and Commerce in Tennessee,' in Mississippi Valley *Historical Review* (December, 1927). It must be understood that these expansions and contractions were not limited to the United States. The young Republic of Mexico was acquiring a debt that was to plague her for years; the Boers of South Africa had started their trek to Transvaal, and Canada and South America were affected by similar expansive forces. See C. R. Fish, 'The Frontier a World Problem,' in Wisconsin *Magazine of History*.

[1] 25th Cong., 2d Sess., *House Ex. Doc.* No. 79, pp. 804–05. Adelaide R. Hasse, *Index to the Economic Material in State Documents — Ohio* (Washington, 1910), serves as an indispensable guide to the collected documents of Ohio. It is one of a series of guides prepared under the auspices of the Library of Congress. For secondary studies of Ohio banking see: C. C. Huntington, 'History of Banking in Ohio before the Civil War,' in Ohio Archeological and Historical Society *Publications*, XXIV; and E. L. Bogart, 'Financial History of Ohio,' in University of Illinois *Studies* (1912), pp. 257–96. A notable characteristic of banking in Ohio before the panic of 1837 was that ordinary speculative business had not been differentiated from banks. This was true of the country as a whole. In Ohio, besides engaging in the export business, banks carried on life insurance, and manufacturing, and ran canals and railroads. Some of these appear not to have been chartered originally for banking purposes, but to have implied note issue privileges from their charters. Other organizations which assumed banking functions were those engaged in 'silk manufacturing.' In one case a library was converted into a 'bank.' These institutions were generally tolerated until a period of distress, when they came to be regarded as subtle 'bank evasions' and suspicion was deepened that bankers were shrewd and clever men. Comparisons were made between these institutions and the Bank of the Manhattan Company, organized by Aaron Burr, for the ostensible purpose of supplying New York City with water. It turned

decreased to twenty-three, of which thirteen were to expire in 1845 and the remaining ten by 1855.[1] In 1845, when the new system went into effect, the number of Ohio banks had decreased to eight with a corresponding shrinkage of capital and circulation. These figures measure the effect of the panic of 1837 on the Ohio banking system.

The movement for reorganization began as a direct result of the panic, and culminated in a new system in 1845. The eight years following the panic was a period, not only of great suspicion of banks, but also of constructive discussion, and the result was a new system better than the old. A committee report to the Legislature showed this constructive thought. On January 14, 1839, Mr. John Brough proposed a bill providing for a board of bank commissioners. Furthermore, it proposed that if at any time the specie reserves of a bank fell below one third of its circulation, or the sum of its deposits and circulation exceeded one hundred and fifty per cent of its capital, directors and stockholders be held individually liable in their private capacities.[2] By an act of February 25, 1839, this plan was partially adopted by creating a board of bank commissioners with powers of inspection.[3] Another committee report, presented by T. W. Bartley, proposed a more sweeping reorganization, stating that the purpose was 'not the destruction but a thorough and radical reformation of the banking system.' It opposed a State bank because it would increase the State debt, and create a 'moneyed power' allied with the Government. It rejected the idea of complete freedom of banking such as the *'free swindling system'* of Michigan on the ground that the public interest required regulation. Its constructive proposal provided for a general uniform law, unlimited director and stockholder liability, a specie reserve equal to one third

out to be a bank, however, in competition with Hamilton's Bank of North America. It still operates under the same name.

[1] 29th Cong., 1st Sess., *House Ex. Doc.* No. 226, p. 1128, *Annual Report of Bank Commissioners*, December 21, 1840. *Ohio Reports*, 1843, Doc. No. 38, pp. 15–17, *Annual Report of Bank Commissioners*, December 17, 1843.

[2] 25th Cong., 3d Sess., *House Ex. Doc.* No. 227, pp. 627–40, text of proposed bill.

[3] Hasse, p. 289.

the circulation, and a safety-fund like the New York System.[1] The first annual report of the bank commissioners declared that the great error of the old system was the lack of individual liability. It argued that banking was affected by such a public interest as to render State regulation imperative, and that the relation of a bank corporation to a bill-holder was such that any theory of *laissez-faire* was impossible to accept.[2] The outcome of this discussion was a general bank law of March 7, 1842, providing that in any future banks organized, directors and shareholders were to be 'held jointly and severally liable.'[3] So severe, however, was this provision that no banks undertook to organize. Governor T. W. Bartley, who had been active in the discussion, declared in his message of December 3, 1844, that the banks regarded these restrictions as too severe. He warned them that a paper-money system was not an absolute necessity, that metallic money could take the place of paper, and that banks as hitherto conducted had tended to 'the opulence of the few and the pauperism of the many.' He was opposed to a free-bank system based on a deposit of bonds since this resulted in an 'unholy coalition' of State and banks, and notes secured by this method could not be kept at par. If paper money was to be retained, a system must be devised whereby it would circulate at par, and the best method to accomplish this was by a specie reserve and loans made on short-time commercial paper.[4] The new Governor, Mordecai Bartley, favored protecting circulation by a specie reserve of one third and a deposit of securities equal to the note issue.[5] The result of all this discussion was a new system provided by the act of February 24, 1845.

This fixed the maximum bank capital of Ohio at $6,150,-

---

[1] 26th Cong., 1st Sess., *House Ex. Doc.* No. 172, pp. 1084-91. This document is undated but it bears internal evidence of being written in 1840.

[2] 29th Cong., 1st Sess., *House Ex. Doc.* No. 226, p. 1135, December 21, 1840.

[3] *Ohio Laws*, 1842, pp. 46-47. This act was amended on February 21, 1843, making the liability clause less severe, *Ohio Laws*, 1843, pp. 36-37.

[4] 29th Cong., 1st Sess., *House Ex. Doc.* No. 226, p. 1162.

[5] *Ibid.*, p. 1172.

000; divided the State into twelve districts; and prescribed the number of banks and the amount of capital for each district. A board of five commissioners was to serve for one year to inaugurate the system, and thereafter the commission was to consist of the Auditor, Treasurer, and Secretary of State. The core of the system was to be a State Bank, capitalized by private subscription, with branches throughout the State. It was to be under the general administration of a central board of control at Columbus, vested with the powers of distributing notes to the branches, inspecting at will, requiring monthly statements of conditions, and ordering a contraction of discounts and circulation if conditions made necessary. Circulation was to be protected by a thirty per cent specie reserve in each vault; and a ten per cent safety-fund contributed by the member banks. This safety-fund might be either specie, or the bonds of the United States or the State of Ohio, and was to be held in trust by the State Treasurer and devoted to the note redemption of insolvent banks. The total circulation of each bank was limited by sliding scale. For the first $100,000 of capital a bank could not issue more than two hundred per cent of its capital, this percentage being progressively reduced with each additional $100,000 of capital. The total debts of a bank could not exceed two thirds of its capital. Banks already in existence could elect to join the system at the expiration of their charters. Independent banks could organize and remain outside the system, in which case their circulation must be secured by a deposit of securities equal to the amount of notes issued and a thirty per cent reserve. All charters were to expire by May 1, 1866.[1] The annual message of Governor Bartley, December 8, 1846, declared the new system was a success, with twenty-six banks in operation — seventeen branches of the State Bank, nine independent banks, and eight still operating under charters of the old system.[2]

Accompanying this movement for a reformation of the Ohio bank system was a demand for the prohibition of

[1] *Laws*, 1844–45, pp. 24–54, *An Act to Incorporate the State Bank of Ohio and Other Banking Companies*, February 24, 1845.

[2] 29th Cong., 2d Sess., *House Ex. Doc.* No. 120, p. 273.

paper-money banks and a return to 'constitutional hard money.' Always a minority viewpoint in Ohio, confined to the Loco-Foco wing of the Democrats, it was unable to block the act of 1845, and gradually weakened with the reviving prosperity of the later forties. It persisted, however, into the fifties and its influence can be seen in the convention which drafted the constitution of 1851. In this convention, with a Democratic majority,[1] no fewer than five 'no-bank' proposals were presented. Popular referendums were proposed on the questions: 'for banks or against banks,' 'hard money or anti-hard money,' and 'banks or no banks.'[2] Another proposal called for the gradual retirement of paper money by 1866, a five-year test period in which only hard money would be used, and a referendum in 1871 on the subject.[3] The majority of the committee on banks and currency reported against banks, arguing that they were unconstitutional either by National or State act. By the Federal Constitution, argued the report, no State could 'emit bills of credit,' and the only power over currency delegated to the Federal Government was to coin money. Quotations were made from *Madison's Notes* tending to show that the Fathers intended to 'crush paper money.' In prohibiting to the States the power to emit bills of credit, and in delegating to the National Government no more than the power to coin money, the Constitution left no room for paper-money banks. The minority report argued in reply that the prohibition of paper money would fall most heavily on the debtor classes by price depression; while one man agreed with the minority but suggested general incorporation as a solution.[4] The final action provided for general incorporation applying to all corporations, although any general bank law must be approved by a popular referendum.[5] The general bank law

[1] Isaac F. Patterson, *Constitutions of Ohio* (Cleveland, 1912), p. 109. The convention was composed of 68 Democrats, 41 Whigs, and 3 Freesoilers.

[2] *Official Report of the Debates and Proceedings of the Ohio State Convention* (Columbus, 1851), pp. 88, 989, 991.

[3] *Ibid.*, p. 1033.   [4] *Ibid.*, pp. 848–50.

[5] Francis Newton Thorpe, *Federal and State Constitutions* (7 vols., Washington, 1909), V, pp. 931–32.

was passed May 29, 1851, a standard free-bank law.[1] By
this act the Ohio system received its final form. In 1861,
however, the State Bank was still the dominant institution
of Ohio.[2]

Another aspect of the Ohio bank system was the voluntary effort to maintain par redemption in the Cincinnati
trade center. Even before the act of 1845 five Cincinnati
banks employed a broker to collect foreign paper and present
it for redemption at the counters of issuing banks.[3] After
the panic of 1857 the Ohio State Bank organized a movement to force par redemption for all currency finding its way
into Cincinnati from western Virginia, Indiana, Kentucky,
and Ohio. This organization, known as the Bank of the
Valley of Ohio, was to serve the same purpose for the currency of the Ohio Valley that the Suffolk Bank had done for
New England. After numerous delays it began operations
in September, 1858, and soon had a redemption balance of
$306,000.[4]

When the National Banking System was adopted, Ohio
banks consisted of three types with principles borrowed from
various sources. The State Bank borrowed its general
organization from Indiana, its safety-fund from New York,
its specie reserve from Louisiana, and its par redemption
from New England. The independent banks borrowed the
principle of circulation protected by securities from New
York and the free banks were modeled on the same system.
As a whole the Ohio system was one of unusual strength,
showing a capacity to borrow and a power to create.

THE INDIANA SYSTEM

The constitution by which Indiana was admitted to the
Union in 1816 forbade any bank except a State Bank and
its branches, although two territorial banks at Madison

---

[1] *Bankers' Magazine*, VI, p. 112.

[2] 36th Cong., 2d Sess., *House Ex. Doc.* No. 77, pp. 244–46, February
1, 1861. Of the fifty-five banks in Ohio thirty-six were branches of the
State Bank with a large preponderance of the total capital and circulation.

[3] 26th Cong., 1st Sess., *House Ex. Doc.* No. 172, p. 1063.

[4] *Bankers' Magazine*, XIII, pp. 144, 154.

and Vincennes were permitted to continue.[1] By act of the
first Legislature, January 1, 1817, the Vincennes bank was
designated as the State Bank with fourteen branches. This
organization, engaging in land speculation and a 'Steam
Mill' at Vincennes, fell a victim to the panic of 1819 and
passed out of existence in 1822. From that time until 1834
Indiana was without banks of issue chartered by the State,
although paper money circulated from the Ohio, Kentucky,
and New Orleans banks.[2] Chastened by her first experiment
and by the example of Kentucky, Indiana produced, in the
midst of the speculative era, a system that was one of the
soundest of the day. This was the State Bank of Indiana
created by an act of January 28, 1834.

In general organization it was a closely organized federation of banks under the general control of a central board at
Indianapolis. Its capital was fixed at $1,600,000 and all of
the ten original branches were mutually liable for the total
debts of the system. The stockholders of each branch were
independent in dividends, although the dividend rate for
each branch was fixed by the central board. Furthermore,
the central board could make inspection at will, control all
paper issues, and, if the condition of any bank warranted,
could close it under a receivership. The bank was to act as
the fiscal agent of the State, which owned half of the stock,
elected the president, and shared in the appointment of the
central officers. For its share of the stock the State issued
five per cent bonds and created a Sinking Fund Commission
to receive dividends and pay interest and principal. Any
surplus was to be devoted to the Common School Fund.
The bank could invest none of its funds in 'goods, wares, or
merchandise'; nor in real estate except such as was necessary
for the transaction of its immediate business, or as came
into its possession through foreclosure. It could make no
loans on the security of its own stock nor on the security

[1] Thorpe, II, pp. 1069-70.

[2] Logan Esarey, in 'State Banking in Indiana,' Indiana University
Studies (1912), and 'First Indiana Banks,' Indiana Magazine of History,
VI, pp. 144-58, describes early ventures of the State. The author fails to
appreciate the free-bank movement, and his broad assertion that it
showed the 'sinister hand of party politics' cannot be accepted.

of one director for another. A minimum fund equal to one sixteenth of the capital was to be accumulated from profits and retained as an undivided surplus, and twelve and one half cents per share on stock owned by individuals was to be collected annually in lieu of taxation and devoted to the Common School Fund. In cases of fraudulent insolvency the president and directors were subject to unlimited liability to creditors; and if any debts remained unsatisfied after the exhaustion of general assets and the entire property of the president and directors, the stockholders were individually liable to an amount equal to their shares. The charter was effective until January 1, 1859, but the bank must go into liquidation on January 1, 1857. The more important provisions may be summarized as: federation of branches under a centralized control, mutual liability of branches for the debts of all, a surplus fund withheld from profits, and a special form of individual liability.[1] The State issued five per cent thirty-year bonds which it sold in the East and Europe for its share of the bank stock.[2] Compared to systems later developed it was manifestly weaker in such matters as a specie reserve, individual stockholder liability, and loan limitations. Yet by conservative management such provisions could be rendered unnecessary. It was

---

[1] *An Act to Establish a State Bank*, January 28, 1834, an appendix to William F. Harding, 'The State Bank of Indiana' in *Journal of Political Economy*, IV (1895), pp. 115–38. This study is reprinted without text of charter in *Sound Currency* (1898), pp. 257–77. The annual report of E. Dumont, President, December 30, 1856, in 34th Cong., 3d Sess., *House Ex. Doc.* No. 87, pp. 216–21, presents a brief historical summary. Hugh McCulloch in *Men and Measures of Half a Century* (New York, 1888), pp. 113–23, discusses this bank from the standpoint of his connections with it as a director on the central board and cashier of the Fort Wayne branch. He says that the stockholders were individually liable and Harding assumes that he meant in all cases. This does not seem probable from the intent of the charter which limited the liability to cases of fraudulent insolvency. The principle of individual stockholder liability as adopted into the National Act did not receive general recognition until adopted as a standard provision of the free-bank acts of the fifties.

[2] 29th Cong., 1st Sess., *House Ex. Doc.* No. 226, p. 1102, *Report of the Commissioners of the Sinking Fund*, December, 1844. These bonds were issued as follows: $500,000 due in 1864; $450,000 due in 1865; and $440,000 due in 1866.

stronger in principles, however, than the Second United States Bank.

The ten branches, originally provided for, went into operation in November, 1834; and before the panic three additional branches were opened in the developing northern part of the State at Fort Wayne, South Bend, and Michigan City.[1] Its condition on the eve of the panic showed a conservative management with a specie reserve of approximately twenty-six per cent of its circulation and deposits (including Government deposits of nearly one and one half millions). In the panic month the general policy of contraction was begun and adhered to fairly consistently through the period of depression.[2] Although the Bank's reserve was strong, the weakness of its condition in a panic is evident. The uncertainty of Government deposits which were being gradually withdrawn, the 'sluggish' discounts, and the loss of public confidence during the panic rendered necessary a temporary suspension of specie payments; which in this case, as in many others, did not mean actual insolvency. Its condition showed that it was sound as far as ultimate redemption and deposit payment were concerned, and behind all its reserves was the additional protection of mutual branch liability. But the immediate exigencies forced partial suspension.[3]

The State Bank of Indiana, like similar organizations of

[1] McCulloch, p. 113. Some of the prominent men besides Hugh McCulloch connected with this bank may be listed: the three Presidents, Samuel Merril, James Morrison, and E. Dumont; the cashier, James M. Ray; J. F. D. Lanier of Madison, later of New York City; Samuel Emison of Vincennes; Demas Deming of Terre Haute; and Calvin Fletcher of Indianapolis.

[2] Harding, pp. 109–11, statistical tables, 1835–51. The condition on April 29, 1837, was as follows: circulation $2,615,275; individual deposits $579,637; Government deposits $1,435,300; specie $1,222,303. It should be noted that this specie was not the surplus fund required by the charter. The surplus was merely a fund withheld from profits for the purpose of strengthening the general assets and could be reinvested.

[3] Ibid., p. 16; J. F. D. Lanier, Sketch of Life (New York, 1877), pp. 14–19; William B. Ridgely, 'Early Banking in the West,' in Trust Companies (1904), I, pp. 381–90. Ridgely relates that Lanier took $80,000 in gold by stage coach to Washington and quotes Secretary Woodbury

the period, became the object of suspicion and investigation in the depression period after the panic. Samuel Merril was aware both of the tightening money market at the close of 1836 and that the bank would probably be fixed upon in the popular mind as, the cause. He attributed the money stringency to the decrease of silver imports from Mexico, the suppression of small notes by several States, the Specie Circular of Jackson, and the fact that specie export 'from Europe has been much counteracted by the Bank of England.' [1] Soon after the panic he warned the branches to expect attack. 'There are many who will throw upon the bank the blame of the present distress,' but he thought that to destroy all banks because some had been unfortunate was a folly equal to destroying canals or railroads on account of some accidents. [2] A warning was needed, for the bank was confronted by a demand from the State for assistance to meet revenue deficits, by stay laws making collections difficult, by specie drains from the Government and noteholders, and a growing suspicion in the popular mind which deepened into hostility as the panic spread. An irrational psychology of depression emerged, a social attitude, which in the language of H. Parker Willis, regarded 'banks as a species of octopus which feeds upon the rest of the commercial world, and in especial regards the farmers as its legitimate prey.' [3] After a long investigation a committee of the Legislature presented a report which for the purpose of illustrating the anti-bank reactions is valuable.

as saying that it was the only bank offering to pay Government deposits. Payment on small deposits was continued.

[1] 25th Cong., 2d Sess., *House Ex. Doc.* No. 79, pp. 785–86, December 16, 1836.

[2] *Ibid.*, pp. 797–98, May 22, 1837.

[3] *Journal of Political Economy*, IV, p. 106, a review of Charles G. Dawes, *Banking System of United States* (1894), a book written at Lincoln, Nebraska, and reflecting somewhat the feelings of a banker who senses this social attitude in the shadow of the panic of 1893. Professor Willis adds 'this point of view is found in its most radical form in the energetic but unsophisticated great West.' Henry Adams, however, after the panic of 1893 confessed 'an uneasy distrust of bankers and State Street,' and Francis Bacon said 'banks will hardly be brooked in regard of certain suspicions.'

This report asserted that out of a total State population of 105,000, the number of borrowers was 4951, of whom six hundred were stockholders and directors who had borrowed slightly less than one half of the total loans. The report estimated that the benefits of bank credit were confined to one twentieth of the population, nearly one half to bank officials, and generally limited to the thirteen towns in which the branches were located. Merchants, constituting one fiftieth of the population, received twice the credit granted to farmers, constituting three fourths of the population.[1] In reply to these charges President Merril stated that the bank was free from politics, that the State board was bi-partisan, and that no complaint had ever reached him of a loan ever having been made or refused on political grounds. 'But,' he concluded, 'if to party contests already sufficiently bitter, there is to be added each year a struggle for "the power of lending money," it will not be difficult to foretell the result.'[2] In December, 1840, Merril reported that loans were distributed approximately as follows: merchants — $1,000,000; farmers — $600,000; manufacturers and mechanics — $610,000; exporters — $723,000; others — $771,000. By April of 1841 he anticipated that exporters, principally engaged in the New Orleans river trade, would receive $1,000,000 additional with decreases among the other groups, especially merchants.[3] Despite these assaults, which diminished with returning prosperity, the bank recovered and lived out its career.

In accordance with its charter, it went into liquidation, January 1, 1857; and its report at that time showed a policy of consistent conservatism. The total surplus fund amounted to $1,265,203 and the annual dividend ranged from eleven to twenty-two and one half per cent. Since its organization in 1834 the dividends earned by the State on its stock had paid interest on the bonds issued and had accumulated the sum of $1,955,461 in the Sinking Fund.

[1] 26th Cong., 1st Sess., *House Ex. Doc.* No. 172, pp. 893–908.

[2] *Ibid.*, pp. 958–70.

[3] 26th Cong., 2d Sess., *House Ex. Doc.* No. 111, pp. 1381–84, December 8, 1840. During the constitutional convention of 1851 a very frequent charge was that the bank had loaned too much money to farmers.

Since the bank stock was at a premium due to the large surplus, it was estimated that its sale would discharge the bonds and leave the State the Sinking Fund as a net profit to be turned in to the School Fund.[1] It had made money for the State, and redeemed its circulation; yet sound as it was generally acknowledged, the Indiana monster could not expect a recharter. That had already been settled by the Constitution of 1851.

The convention which drafted the Constitution of 1851 consisted of ninety-five Democrats and fifty-five Whigs; and was in session from October 7, 1850, to February 1, 1851.[2] Three clearly defined viewpoints developed; those favoring a State bank, free banks, and no banks. The free-bank proposal was tabled by a vote of 89 to 43, and the State bank proposal by a vote of 75 to 57;[3] indicating that the free-bank group held balance of power. Robert Dale Owen, among others, was a champion of the free-bank system; although he objected to the implications of unregulated banking, and preferred the term 'restricted or general system.' Furthermore, he recognized the defect of the New York system in that it allowed real estate mortgages which though they 'ultimately may be good, immediately they are not.' He recognized, also, that the existing State Bank was a sound institution, but stated that his chief objection to it was that it was a monopoly. He was careful to add, however, that he used the word 'not in its odious sense but in its strict technical sense.' In this sense he regarded the disestablishment of the United States Bank by Andrew Jackson as justifiable. Moreover, he had some sympathy for the no-bank view, particularly as banks had hitherto been conducted. Although credit money, he thought, was necessary and valuable, banking should be conducted without mono-

[1] 34th Cong., 3d Sess., *House Ex. Doc.* No. 87, pp. 218–19, December 30, 1856. No exact estimate of the amount of the present School Fund of Indiana derived from the profits of this bank can be made. It is obvious that it would be more than the approximate $2,000,000 reported in 1856. Harding says that the amount ultimately realized 'was largely in excess of three million and a half of dollars.'

[2] Charles Kettleborough, I, p. 221.

[3] *Report of the Debates and Proceedings* (2 vols., Indianapolis, 1850), II, pp. 1445–47.

poly.[1] His definite proposal was the New York system further strengthened by reserving to the Legislature the right to repeal or modify any charter and the exclusion of real estate mortgages. His argument was drawn largely from Fillmore's report of 1848 and he took to task some of the Whig advocates of the State Bank for failing to appreciate the argument of their Whig President.[2]

The final action of the convention was a combination of the State bank and free-bank views. A bank with branches might be created by special act, with mutual branch responsibility for notes; but the State could not be a stockholder. A free-bank system might be created under a general law with a note issue protected by a deposit with State officers of 'ample collateral security, readily convertible into specie.' In both systems the billholder had priority of interest and stockholders were individually liable.[3]

The act authorizing the free-bank system passed the Legislature May 28, 1852. The basis of circulation was Indiana five per cent stock, or United States six per cent bonds, or six per cent bonds of any State paying its interest regularly. Stockholders were individually liable and a twelve and a half per cent specie reserve was to be maintained against notes.[4] Free banks organized under this law got into difficulty on account of 'wildcat' individuals organizing banks in remote places and using depreciated bonds of other States. In some cases bonds bought by these irresponsible speculators at from fifteen to fifty per cent were used to issue Indiana free-bank currency. The branches of the State Bank, moreover, contributed to the failure of many of these organizations by collecting their paper and presenting it at their counters for redemption.[5] The annual

[1] *Report of the Debates and Proceedings* (2 vols., Indianapolis, 1850), II, pp. 1449–52.

[2] *Ibid.*, pp. 1495, 1511–17. It should be noted, however, that some of the Democrats favored a State bank. Thomas A. Hendricks, later Governor and vice-presidential candidate, was a member of this convention and opposed to free banking. He preferred a chartered monopoly under private ownership.

[3] Thorpe, II, 1088–89.

[4] Indiana *Acts*, 1855, pp. 23–33.

[5] Esarey, pp. 282–84.

message of the Governor in 1853 declared that the system was a failure. 'The speculator,' he said, 'comes to Indianapolis with a bundle of bank notes in one hand and his stock in the other. In twenty-four hours he is on his way to some distant part of the Union to circulate what he denominates a legal currency, authorized by Legislature of the State of Indiana.'[1] The Auditor-General advocated the creation at Indianapolis of a central agency of redemption and, although no legislative action was taken, the State Bank attempted to stabilize the currency by a forced redemption and by coöperating with the Cincinnati banks.[2] In order to remedy these defects an amendment to the free-bank law was enacted over the veto of the Governor in March, 1855. The system was strengthened by the provisions that eleven persons were necessary to organize a bank, that $6,000,000 be the aggregate limit of currency issue, and that stock used as a basis of circulation must be six per cent stock taken at a ratio of one hundred ten to one hundred.[3] After the enactment of these restrictions the free banks regained public confidence,[4] but in 1861 they were still of less importance than the Bank of the State of Indiana.[5]

The Bank of the State of Indiana was created March 3, 1855, under the provision of the constitution permitting a bank with branches in addition to free banks. It was privately owned, had a twenty-year charter, and was authorized to establish from fifteen to twenty branches. Stockholders were individually liable for the debts of the whole system and all branches were mutually responsible.[6] The organization of this 'little monster,' although clearly permitted by the constitution, was the occasion for a renewed bank war. Governor Joseph A. Wright charged in a message to the Legislature that its charter had been secured through the fraudulent distribution of stock and voting of ab-

[1] *Bankers' Magazine*, VII, pp. 667; 739–40.

[2] 33d Cong., 2d Sess., *House Ex. Doc.* No. 82, p. 208.

[3] Indiana *Acts*, 1855, pp. 33–48.

[4] 34th Cong., 3d Sess., *House Ex. Doc.* No. 87, p. 213.

[5] 37th Cong., 3d Sess., *House Ex. Doc.* No. 1161, p. 164. The total capital of the eighteen free banks in 1861 was $1,226,935.

[6] *Acts*, 1855, pp. 229–51.

sentees.[1] He carried the fight to the Supreme Court of the
State in an attempt to have the charter annulled but the
Court declared it legal,[2] and President Hugh McCulloch
denied any fraud in the method by which the charter had
passed the Legislature.[3] At the outbreak of the Civil War,
it was larger than all the eighteen free banks together, having a capital of over $3,000,000 and a circulation of nearly
$6,000,000.[4] It was from the presidency of this bank that
Hugh McCulloch was called to Washington as Comptroller
of the Currency under the National Banking System.

DIVORCE OF BANK AND STATE IN ILLINOIS

By the Constitution of 1818, no banks were to be created
by Illinois, except a State bank and its branches; although
various organizations created by the Territory were to continue.[5] In 1837 there were two banks in the State, both
operating under charters of February 12, 1835. The Bank
of Illinois at Shawneetown, one of the territorial banks
which had failed in 1823, was revived. Since by virtue of the
constitution it could not be given a new charter, its original
charter of December 28, 1816, was revived, amended, and
extended to January 1, 1857. Although by the original

[1] 34th Cong., 3d Sess., *House Ex. Doc.* No. 87, pp. 214–15. Esarey
attaches some weight to the charges, especially in the matter of public
subscription of the stock. It appears that the stock was subscribed by
those already controlling the State Bank, and that others were prevented
from subscribing by closing the books within ten minutes after they were
opened. McCulloch admits that it was controlled by the old State Bank.
The anti-bank forces came to regard it as another bank subtlety.

[2] *Bankers' Magazine*, XIII, p. 825.   [3] *Ibid.*, XII, p. 152.

[4] 37th Cong., 3d Sess., *House Ex. Doc.* 1161, p. 164.

[5] Thorpe, II, 983. Four organizations at Cairo, Edwardsville, Shawneetown, and Kaskaskia operating under charters from the Territory
failed in the depression. The Bank of Cairo, chartered January 9, 1818,
was not organized until 1836, when it revived just before the panic,
issued a number of notes, failed, and was placed in liquidation by an act
of March 3, 1843. The history of these early banks is discussed in George
William Dowrie, *Development of Banking in Illinois* (1913); Charles
Hunter Garnett, *State Banks of Issue in Illinois* (1898); and Theodore
Calvin Pease, *The Frontier State*, in *Centennial History of Illinois*, II
(1918). A. R. Hasse, *Index to the Economic Material in State Documents
— Illinois* (1909), provides a guide to the Illinois documents for the en-
tire period.

charter $100,000 of its capital stock was reserved to the Territory, the stock had not been subscribed. By the amended charter of 1835, however, the State accepted the stock and arranged for its sale at public auction on May 1, 1835, the expected premium to go to the State treasury. In lieu of all taxation a bonus of one half per cent on its capital was payable annually to the State.[1] It remained a small bank engaged, as it had formerly been, in the New Orleans river trade and the import of Eastern manufactures.[2] Before the panic, however, it was converted from a small institution based on the river trade into an agency for the gigantic internal improvement ventures of the State. The conclusion of the Black Hawk War and the thrust of immigration to the central and northern portions of the State drew this bank into the maelstrom of land speculation and internal improvements. It was authorized to borrow $250,000 and loan it on real estate mortgages; to increase its capital by the sum of $1,400,000 (all of which was reserved to the State); and to extend branches to Jacksonville, Alton, and Lawrenceville.[3] It was thus definitely made both a State and a speculative institution and its failure in the panic was a foregone conclusion.

The other organization was the State Bank of Illinois at Springfield. By its charter, effective to January 1, 1860, it was to have $1,500,000 capital, of which the State reserved to itself $100,000. Its main office was to be located at Springfield, with branches at Vandalia and five other towns. It might borrow $1,000,000 and loan on real estate mortgages.[4] It is clear that even before it became an agency of internal improvement in 1837, it was much more speculative than its sister institutions of Indiana and Missouri. The large loans which it was authorized to make on real estate mortgages established its connection with land specu-

---

[1] *Laws*, 1835, pp. 15–22.

[2] 24th Cong., 2d Sess., *House Ex. Doc.* No. 65, pp. 164–5.

[3] *Laws*, 1837, pp. 17–18.

[4] *Laws*, 1835, pp. 7–14. The State President was Thomas Mather and the cashier, Nicholas H. Ridgely. Its branches were located at Vandalia, Alton, Chicago, Jacksonville, Galena, and Mount Carmel. Three other branches were subsequently authorized.

lation. Moreover, it not only lacked all the conservative principles of the State Bank of Indiana, such as mutual branch responsibility, centralized control, a surplus fund, and a low circulation and discount line; but it was made still more speculative in March just before the panic. The Governor was 'authorized and required' to subscribe for the $100,-000 of stock reserved by the charter and its capital was increased $2,000,000, all of which was subscribed by the State.[1]

There was little in future developments to justify the report of the legislative committee that 'the condition of the State Bank of Illinois is sound, and its credit firmly established.'[2] The panic in May brought suspension, investigation, and suspicion. The farmer, faced with fixed interest charges and a principal difficult to renew, and who found himself paid for his produce with depreciating paper in a falling market, convinced himself that banks were by nature swindling institutions. The State, with a revenue system adjusted to the expectation of large profits from its bank investments and internal improvement ventures, and confronted with heavy interest charges and a depleted treasury, became convinced that the proper policy was a separation of bank and State.

After suspending in company with other banks of the country in 1837, the State Bank temporarily resumed; but a second suspension was ordered on October 23, 1839. President Mather, noting that many reports were current reflecting on the bank, called attention to the fact that, although by the charter a suspension of sixty days was cause for forfeiture of the charter, he considered that an enforcement of this forfeiture would cause great distress. It would force the bank to press debtors for the collection of loans and sell State bonds in its possession.[3] In order to determine whether suspension of specie payments was to be legalized, a joint committee of eight was appointed to investigate the bank. Four of these, including Abraham Lincoln, one of the Sangamon 'long nine,' presented a report defending the bank.

[1] *Laws*, 1837, pp. 18–22. Acts of March 2 and March 4, 1837.

[2] *Senate Journal*, 1836–37, p. 442, February 16, 1837.

[3] 26th Cong., 1st Sess., *House Ex. Doc.* No. 172, pp. 869–71. December 8, 1839.

The charter, declared the report, was legally forfeited but suspension had been forced upon the bank by the action of eastern banks and was not equivalent to insolvency. Regarding the charges that the loans of the bank were unduly extended to non-residents, surprise was expressed 'at the smallness of the business which the Bank has done with non-residents.' The largest non-resident loan was to Samuel Wiggins on the pledge of his own stock in the bank. This was bad judgment but the practice was not a general one with the bank. A loan to Godfrey, Gilam and Company, of Alton, although 'swollen to immense amount of $800,748,' was now reduced and was on safe security. Such a large loan, however, to one firm was bad policy, since it served 'to engender heart burnings and to enlist enemies,' and to excite the people about 'the privileges and powers of banks.' Such a large loan to T. Biddle had been the cause of much suspicion against the United States Bank. In advancing money to Alton commission merchants there had been bad judgment but the purpose had been to divert the lead trade from St. Louis to Alton.[1] A second report by three members of the committee was less favorable. The State owned $2,100,000 of the $3,644,655 of capital, yet had only five of the fourteen directors; and citizens of Illinois owned but $63,120 of the stock. The rest of the stock was in the hands of non-residents, of which 'Samuel Wiggins, of the city of Cincinnati,' held nine hundred shares and had been permitted to borrow a large sum on the security of his own stock. Yet the total loans to non-residents were less than the committee 'had expected to find.' By extending large loans to lead merchants of Alton and pork dealers of Chicago, the bank had tended to favor particular sections of the State. The salaries of the bank officials were too large in comparison with those of State officials and the second suspension was unwarranted.[2] Richard Murphy, of Cook County, reported separately, bitterly denouncing bankers and men of wealth in general.[3] As a result of this investiga-

[1] *Illinois Reports*, 1839–40, pp. 243–51, January 21, 1840.

[2] *Ibid.*, pp. 253–59. The list of stockholders shows Wiggins with 900 shares as the largest, p. 356.

[3] *Ibid.*, pp. 260–68.

tion the suspension was legalized and the charter continued.[1]

At the close of 1840, however, the bank was again in difficulty. It had resumed December 5, on the expectation of general resumption which had not occurred, and great drains on its specie resulted. Furthermore, it was advancing to the State for about one half of its current expenses. Mather suggested, therefore, with the concurrence of the directors, that the Legislature legalize a third suspension. To continue redemption, he thought, it would be necessary to sell State bonds in the bank's possession, cease further advances to the State, and curtail its circulation and loans. Such a policy would depress prices and further aggravate the distress.[2] This proposal resulted in an explosion of anti-bank wrath which within two years forced the banks into liquidation. In reply a minority committee report presented by Richard Murphy declared: 'We stand before the world, in the attitude of men professing republican equality, and at the same time cherishing and fostering by law the most inexorable species of aristocracy that ever was recognized in any age or nation....' Bankers, it was thought, 'by the erection of banks and other paper fabrications, adopt means to banish precious metals from the country, and substitute therefor, pieces of paper, *merely promises to pay*, which possess no intrinsic value.... The Israelites of old erected a golden calf and worshiped it. The object of our idolatry is not gold but paper.'[3]

The State Treasury in the meantime was in such desperate straits that it was delinquent on its interest in January, 1842.[4] It scarcely had specie enough to get its letters from the United States post office, and the payment of taxes in the depreciated bills of the two banks threatened still further to reduce the revenue. On August 15, 1842, therefore, a joint proclamation was issued by the Governor, Auditor, and Treasurer, ordering that, after September 12, the notes of the State Bank be refused in payment of taxes or interest

[1] 26th Cong., 1st Sess., *House Ex. Doc.* No. 172, p. 883, January 31, 1840.

[2] 29th Cong., 1st Sess., *House Ex. Doc.* No. 226, pp. 1013–16, December 15, 1840; p. 1023, February 6, 1841.

[3] *Ibid.*, pp. 1028–37, February 22, 1841.   [4] *Ibid.*, p. 1048.

on the school fund. On September 12, another order was issued against receiving the notes of the Bank of Illinois at more than their current specie value for the same purposes.[1] Governor Thomas Carlin in his final message recommended repeal of the charters. 'The powers,' said he, 'of a succeeding Legislature to repeal any act of a preceding one, affecting the public interest, results from the nature of our institutions.' This was, he thought, 'the only effective security of the rights of individuals against the invasions of corporate bodies,' any theory of 'vested rights' to the contrary notwithstanding.[2] The new Governor, Thomas Ford, however, proposed the more moderate course of first ordering resumption; and upon failure to comply, placing the banks in gradual liquidation.[3] A joint resolution of the Legislature directed the Governor, Auditor and Fund Commissioner to negotiate the terms of a separation between bank and State. Mather, president of the State Bank, gave notice of a willingness to divorce. He proposed an exchange of evidences of State debt held by the bank for bank stock held by the State. He desired, however, that permission be given to attempt resumption by August 1, 1843; and if successful the continuation of the bank as a private institution. He reported that the bank held evidences of State debt in an amount of $2,152,404, consisting of bonds, script, and advances to the State. The State held $2,100,000 of the bank's stock, so that an equal exchange would leave the State still indebted to the bank.[4] An exchange of securities was made, but the bank was not allowed to continue except in liquidation. By an act of January 24, 1843, entitled; 'An Act to Diminish the State Debt and Put the State Bank in Liqui-

[1] 29th Cong., 1st Sess., *House Ex. Doc.* No. 226, p. 1044; 1047. It was in connection with these orders that Lincoln's Aunt Rebecca letter, satirizing auditor James Shields, was published in the *Sangamon Journal*, August 27, 1842. This satire resulted in what Lincoln described as a 'quasi duel' with Shields. Furthermore, it resulted in reconciliation and marriage with his fellow conspirator, Miss Mary Todd. (Nicolay and Hay, I, pp. 221–31.)

[2] *Ibid.*, p. 1050, December 7, 1842.

[3] *Ibid.*, p. 1052, December 8, 1842.

[4] 29th Cong., 1st Sess., *House Ex. Doc.* No. 226, pp. 1039–40. December 21, 1842.

dation,' commissioners were created to wind up its affairs.[1]
On February 8, 1843, Governor Ford announced that the
exchange had been effected; that the 'odious connexion between bank and State' was dissolved; and that the following day some $2,000,000 of State debt would be destroyed
before the State House in the presence of the General Assembly.[2]

In the meantime, similar arrangements were being effected
with the Bank of Illinois. The State held $1,000,000 of
bank stock and the bank held $370,818 in evidences of
State debt, consisting of bonds, script, and various advances
to the State including a loan to build the new state house.[3]
The bank was willing to divorce by an exchange but wished
to continue under its charter. The majority report of the
committee considering this proposal, presented by Richard
Murphy, was a lengthy and bitter anti-bank document. The
cause of the present distress was the paper banking system
by which 'the industry of the many is appropriated for the
benefit of the few' — a system of 'nobles, without titles,'
which it was estimated had 'extracted from the people of
this country' over one billion dollars in bank failures. The
solution was the 'expulsion of all paper money,' and the
immediate liquidation of the Bank of Illinois at Shawneetown. The minority agreed with so much of the report as
recommended liquidation which, indeed, was only the last
few lines of a remarkable document.[4] On February 25, 1843,
the Bank of Illinois was placed in liquidation by an act
entitled; 'An Act to Diminish the State Debt by One Million Dollars and Put the Bank of Illinois in Liquidation.'[5]

[1] Hasse, p. 116. It was to have until March 4, 1847, to liquidate, but
by act of March 1, 1847, this was extended to November 1, 1848, after
which the Governor was to appoint three trustees to take charge. These
trustees did not complete their work until 1863.

[2] 29th Cong., 1st Sess., *House Ex. Doc.* No. 226, pp. 1081–82.

[3] *Ibid.*, pp. 54–55. January 16, 1843, report of James Dunlap, Agt.

[4] *Ibid.*, pp. 1058–79; 1088. January 20, 1843. One detects, however,
a note of satire in the minority reference to Murphy's report as a 'political and *philosophical* history of banking in the United States, England,
France, Cuba, and other portions of the world for more than the last
hundred years.'

[5] Hasse, p. 111.

Two days later, Governor Ford announced that he had received $500,000 of State debt which had been destroyed, and that the remaining $500,000 was to be delivered and destroyed by February 27, 1844. Thus, as a contemporary Chicago attorney wrote the epitaphs, 'all the Banks in Illinois have ceased to be.' [1] And so it was until 1851 when the free-bank system went into operation after a long bank war — a subject reserved for another chapter.

THE STATE BANK OF MISSOURI

The first Missouri Constitution provided that the General Assembly could create 'one banking company, and no more'; with a maximum capital of $5,000,000, at least one half of which was reserved to the State.[2] It was not, however, until 1837 that action was taken to create a State Bank. In the meantime, Missouri was not without experience; for before 1837, four institutions existed. Two of these, the Bank of St. Louis and the Bank of Missouri, had been created by the Territory, and passed out of existence in the depression following the panic of 1819. The Loan Office, organized in 1821 as a relief measure, was based on capital furnished by the State and loaned on real estate mortgages; but it was declared unconstitutional by the United States Supreme Court in the case of Craig *vs.* Missouri. The agency of the Commercial Bank of Cincinnati, established at St. Louis in 1835 to receive Government deposits, was forced out in 1837 when the State Bank was created.[3] It

[1] Henry Brown, *History of Illinois* (New York, 1844), p. 428. As late as 1854, Ford declared that 'banking cannot succeed except in a state of settled organized society....' *History of Illinois* (1854), p. 173.

[2] Thorpe, IV, p. 2161.

[3] John Ray Cable, 'The Missouri State Bank,' Columbia University *Studies*, CII (1923), pp. 17–95; 149–57 — an exhaustive study of Missouri State banking. Other secondary accounts dealing with these early banks are: Breckenridge Jones, 'One Hundred Years of Banking in Missouri,' in *Missouri Historical Review*, XV (1921); F. F. Stephens, 'Banking and Finance in Missouri in the Thirties,' Mississippi Valley Historical Association, *Proceedings*, X (1917); and Albert J. McCullough, 'The Loan Office Experiment,' University of Missouri Social Science Studies (1914). Moses Austin who lost money in the Bank of Missouri, and who declared his stock in the Bank of St. Louis was 'not worth a Cent,' 'left Missouri about the 1st of May, 1820,' for Texas.

issued no paper, but did a large loan and discount business.[1]

From the passing of the Bank of Missouri about 1821, no regular bank of issue was created by the State until 1837. This at first thought may appear to be strange, for it was a period of great bank expansion elsewhere, and St. Louis was the trade center of the upper Mississippi Valley. To and from her markets came the wagon trains of Sante Fé, the fur traders of the West, the lead dealers of Galena, and the steam boats of the river trade. Explanation, perhaps, is found in the facts that much Mexican silver came from Sante Fé;[2] that a branch of the United States Bank existed at St. Louis; and that Thomas Hart Benton, formerly a director but now no friend of banks, was a dominant figure in Missouri politics.

A movement to create a bank under the provisions of the Constitution was resisted by Governor Daniel Dunklin. Paper money banks, he declared, constituted a 'system of legalized swindling.' The people, moreover, were 'opposed to all banks; and their objections based on former Missouri experience seem well founded.'[3] In his message of November 18, 1834, he declared that the 'whole system of paper money' was inexpedient, and, 'when stock holders of banks are not individually responsible for the redemption of the notes they issue, dangerous to the best interests of the people.' The following January, however, he was willing to accept a bank of discount and deposit, or even a bank of issue if stockholders were made individually responsible and the profits devoted to education.[4] Bills drawn on this sug-

American Historical Association *Annual Report* (1919), II, Pt. I, pp. 3; 385.

[1] 25th Cong., 2d Sess., *House Ex. Doc.* No. 79, pp. 842–43. In January, before being forced out in June, 1837, it had $1,398,811 in loans and $2,262,900 in deposits.

[2] F. F. Stephens, 'Missouri and the Sante Fé Trade,' *Missouri Historical Review*, XI (1917).

[3] Cable, p. 114, January 14, 1834.

[4] *Messages and Proclamations of the Governors of the State of Missouri* (6 vols., 1922–24), I, pp. 242; 294. This idea is obviously Benton's, for in his speech (attacking the United States Bank) February 2, 1831, he declared that exemption of stockholders from individual liability was un-

gestion, however, failed of passage. Governor L. W. Boggs, an ex-cashier of the defunct Bank of Missouri, was more favorable. Although he considered banks to be 'anti-republican in spirit and tendency,' total exclusion he deemed impracticable, and therefore recommended a State Bank.[1] Following this came an act of February 2, 1837, creating the State Bank of Missouri.

The charter, effective to 1857, authorized a capital of $5,000,000, one half of which was reserved to the State. The president and one half of the directors of the central board were elected by the General Assembly. Circulation was limited to one hundred per cent of its capital during the first five years of its operation with the privilege of increasing it thereafter to two hundred per cent of the capital. A twenty per cent interest penalty was placed on suspended bills, and redemption centers were to be located at New Orleans and in the East.[2] As a type, it was similar to the Indiana State Bank; yet a comparison of the two shows it to be weaker than its prototype.

It began operations on May 10, 1837, and was fortunate in failing to get its business expanded before the panic.[3] It was fortunate also, in the conservatism of its officers. With John Brady Smith as president, Henry Shurlds as cashier, and John O'Fallon, ex-manager of the St. Louis branch of the United States Bank as one of the directors, it was served by men of caution and experience.[4] It refused to expand its circulation or extend its loans unduly in the depression period. A difficult problem presented itself as to what should be done with the rapidly depreciating money

just. 'The true principle in banking requires each stock holder to be liable to the amount of his shares...' a restriction which he said, 'has prevailed in Scotland for the last century.' *Abridgment of Debates*, XI, p. 155. This idea was, indeed, some twenty years ahead of its time for America. Cable credits Benton with a more constructive attitude than he is commonly supposed to have had and suggests that much of the conservatism of the Missouri State Bank was due to his influence.

[1] *Messages, etc.*, pp. 313–17, Nov. 22, 1836.　　[2] Cable, pp.134–64.

[3] 25th Cong., 2d Sess., *House Ex. Doc.* No. 79, pp. 842–43. On September 16, 1837, only $28,000 in circulation was reported; January 1, 1838, $94,000, and January 1, 1839, $641,950.

[4] Cable, pp. 164–68.

of the Illinois banks, with which much of the St. Louis
business was carried on. In November, 1839, it issued an
order refusing to receive such money; and although it was
sustained by the Legislature, the bank encountered much
opposition from some St. Louis merchants, who retaliated
by withdrawing their deposits and causing a run. It adhered
to its policy, however, until March 12, 1841, when the order
was rescinded.[1] There was some difficulty in disposing of
State bonds, due both to the distress of the times and defects
in the charter. The charter was amended, requiring an
annual surplus accumulation equal to one per cent of the
capital, and making the bonds bear six per cent interest
payable in London. These changes, however, failed to bring
about an immediate sale of bonds. Frederick Huth and
Company, the London firm to which the bonds had been
sent for sale, called attention to the low prices on 'American
securities,' and stated that 'the attention of our capitalists,
and others engaged in American affairs is now turned to
your internal politics....' The firm was unable to purchase
or advance on the bonds; although, if 'your election for the
Presidentship should have the result now anticipated, it is
very possible that an impulse will be given to all State
stocks....'[2]

The bank faced some suspicion which, however, appears
to have been less violent than in Illinois. The report of the
committee of investigation in 1838 showed little of the anti-
bank violence of other States; its greatest complaint being
the need '*to lend money in small sums to small dealers,*' instead of large loans.[3] Another report found no reasons for

[1] 29th Cong., 1st Sess., *House Ex. Doc.* No. 226, pp. 989–96. The
Sante Fé traders sent $45,000 of silver to assist in the run of 1839. In
fact its specie was largely composed of silver, over four times as much
silver as gold. 26th Cong., 1st Sess., *House Ex. Doc.* No. 172, p. 868.

[2] 26th Cong., 2d Sess., *House Ex. Doc.* No. 111, pp. 1377–78. Letters
to John Brady Smith January 3, and September 11, 1840. As late as
1844 some $2,230,000 of these six per cent bonds were still unsold. 29th
Cong., 1st Sess., *House Ex. Doc.* No. 226, p. 999, September, 1844.

[3] 25th Cong., 3d Sess., *House Ex. Doc.* No. 227, pp. 604–10, November,
1838. Since it commends Benton's policies, the judgment would seem
fair that it represented the anti-bank view. The most significant part
of the report, however, is its explanation of the panic: 'the first blow

the various rumors of favoritism in loans either to city over
rural or large over small borrowers; for ninety per cent of
rural applications had been granted against fifty per cent of
the urban.[1] During the suspension wave of 1839–40, Governor Boggs spoke of the bank as a 'barrier and an exception';[2] and a joint committee report spoke of it as a system
well conducted. Although the State was making no money
on its investments in 1844, its management was referred to as
cautious and was only then expanding its circulation. During this same period it had made considerable loans to
the State to build the new capitol and wage 'the Mormon
War.'[3]

By 1845, the depression period being over, it began
cautiously to expand; and throughout the fifties gained a
reputation as the 'Gibraltar of the West.' Its reports for
the years following showed a steadily growing surplus, large
reserves, and conservative dividends.[4] Its charter expired in
1857, but it was extended and made to conform to the general law of that year. The State, however, contrary to the
general trend, still kept a large investment.[5] On January 1,
1862, the State had an investment of $1,086,300 against a
private investment of $2,332,302.[6] The Constitution of
1865, however, provided for the sale of the State's interest.[7]
This was bought by James B. Eads for $1,178,635.50,[8] and
the State went definitely out of the banking business; the
Bank of the State of Missouri, however, continuing under
the National System. During all this period the little monster encountered the opposition of those groups wishing
which the trader received was from the Bank of England,' which with-
drew credit from American houses, 'and forced them to exact prompt
payment from their American debtors.'

[1] Cable, p. 174.

[2] 26th Cong., 2d Sess., *House Ex. Doc.* No. 111, pp. 1375–77. November 17, 1840.

[3] 29th Cong., 1st Sess., *House Ex. Doc.* No. 226, pp. 993–94; 1003–07.

[4] Cable, pp. 190–98.

[5] *Messages and Proclamations of the Governors of the State of Missouri,*
III, pp. 89–91. Message of R. M. Stewart, October 29, 1858.

[6] 36th Cong., 2d Sess., *House Ex. Doc.* No. 77, p. 178.

[7] Thorpe, IV, p. 2212.

[8] Cable, p. 291.

either no banks, free banks, or private monopolies — a discussion deferred to a subsequent chapter.

In the meantime, however, the monopoly of the State Bank gave way to a general system in the fifties. By an amendment of the Constitution the General Assembly was empowered to establish such banks and branches as it deemed necessary; subject to the limitations that each bank must be 'based upon a specie capital,' no more than ten might be created, and that the total capital not exceed twenty million dollars.[1] The general law of March 2, 1857, provided for a reorganization. The Bank of the State was continued with seven branches; and other large institutions were created at St. Louis with internal branches. Independent banks were chartered for Lexington and St. Joseph; but banking capital was still concentrated at St. Louis, and the Bank of the State remained the largest in the State. The most important feature of the general law of 1857 was the requirement that all banks keep a thirty-three and one third per cent reserve against circulation. It should be noted that this was not a free-bank system of the New York type, but more nearly resembled the Louisiana system.[2] It was characteristic of Missouri that it drew its principles both from the Northwest and the Cotton South.

[1] Thorpe, IV, p. 2174.

[2] *Bankers' Magazine*, XI, pp. 757; 820–24. It did provide for a contingent fund reserved from profits and invested in State bonds; and, also, that a certain proportion of its capital should be invested in such bonds. Such funds, however, were not held in trust by State authorities.

CHAPTER IV

BANKING IN THE LOWER SOUTH

IN that portion of the Old South, aptly called the Cotton
Kingdom, the Jacksonian era witnessed a phenomenon of
fundamental importance. This was the social and economic
revolution caused by the drive of the plantation system into
the rich cotton lands of the lower South. 'King Cotton,'
which displaced the older staples of rice, indigo, and tobacco
in the thirties, became the largest single export of the Nation
and the economic basis of the Cotton Belt. This economic
revolution was not merely American, but was a world phenomenon, represented by the spindle at Manchester, the
cotton bale at New Orleans, and the calico bolt at Calcutta.
Besides affecting attitudes on the tariff and slavery, shifting
commercial centers from Charleston and Savannah to
Mobile and New Orleans, pushing the small farmer to
Texas and the uplands, and stimulating the New Orleans
river trade, it powerfully influenced the banking history of
the lower South. Joined to the normal urge for State aid to
internal improvements was the desire for credit to develop
the large plantations. The types of banks, therefore, became
the land banks and the improvement banks, both of which
met disaster in the panic of 1837. The land banks, founded
on capital borrowed in Europe on State credit and designed
to lend on real estate mortgages, found themselves in the
period of distress unable to realize quickly on their assets
in order to meet demands for note redemption and deposit
payment. 'The only safeguard against bankruptcy brought
about by a sudden run is an adequate specie reserve, and a
set of assets that can be realized in short time. Best of all
assets is commercial paper, running for short periods of 30,
60, or 90 days.' [1] Nowhere in the cotton area was the credit

[1] F. L. Paxson, *The History of the American Frontier* (New York,
1924), p. 234. 'Let us coin our lands, and thereby obtain from these
most valuable of all mines, a sufficient circulating medium of commerce,'
wrote a pamphleteer of 1786. It was neither the first nor the last time

pressure more powerful, nor the results on banking more disastrous, than in Mississippi — the premier Cotton State.

THE MISSISSIPPI BUBBLE

By the Mississippi Constitution of 1817, at least one fourth of the capital of any bank must be reserved for State subscription.[1] The Bank of Mississippi, created by the Territory in 1809, was shortly converted by the State into the Bank of the State of Mississippi, an institution very similar to the other State monopolies of the period. As the cotton plantation began to dominate the economic life of Mississippi, banking reacted violently to the new forces; and the State entered a new phase with land and improvement banks the prevailing type. The Bank of the State of Mississippi was placed in liquidation and the Planters' Bank of Natchez took its place in 1830.[2] By the original charter and an amendment of 1833, the Planters' Bank was capitalized by the proceeds of a $2,000,000 State bond issue. The expectation was that the profits derived from State stock would pay all interest on bonds and accumulate a sinking fund to retire them at maturity.[3] With about a five per cent

the advice was given. Benjamin Franklin in 1729 thought the traditional 'stability of land' offered a suitable security for paper, the Massachusetts Land Bank of 1740 had been notorious, and even Hamilton was at one time drawn to the land security idea. His report of 1790, however, gave the classic argument against it. (Miller, *Banking Theories before 1860,* pp. 125–30.) Moreover, the Michigan 'wildcats' were founded on this principle, Illinois banks were involved in land speculation, and Silas M. Stilwell was urging the idea on New York. The large amount of mortgage security permitted by the free-bank law of 1838 may, indeed, have come from this pressure for agricultural credit.

[1] Thorpe, IV, p. 2004.

[2] Charles Hillman Brough, 'The History of Banking in Mississippi,' in Mississippi Historical Society *Publications,* III (1904), pp. 317–20; Dunbar Rowland, *Encyclopedia of Mississippi History* (2 vols., Madison, Wis., 1907), I, pp. 181–207; R. W. Millsap, 'History of Banking in Mississippi,' in *Sound Currency,* X (1898).

[3] Alexander Trotter, *Observations on the Financial Position and Credit of Such States of the North American Union As Have Contracted Public Debts* (London, 1839), p. 306, a convenient investor's manual. The $300,000 issued in 1830 came due in four equal installments on December 16, of the years 1840, 1845, 1851, and 1856. The $1,500,000 issued in 1833 came due in three equal installments on March 1 of the years

specie reserve and frozen assets, it was natural that the
panic toppled this unstable financial structure into ruins,
and the liability of the bonds issued devolved on the State
under its pledge of faith.[1]

The creation of the Planters' Bank inaugurated a series of
internal improvement corporations with banking privileges,
and launched the State on a career of frenzied finance, which
equaled that of Michigan and Illinois in the same period.
Banks were chartered with reckless abandon to build railroads and waterworks, the ratio of specie to circulation and
deposits was at a most conservative estimate no greater
than one to fifteen, and public inspection was of the most
inadequate sort.[2] The bank commissioners, created after
the panic, suggested as a reform measure the requirement
of a specie reserve of from one fourth to one third; and
called attention to the deposit threat, not generally understood until after the panic of 1857. Mississippi banks,
thought the commissioners, needed more specie reserve
than a State like Louisiana, on account of the lack of
diversified agriculture which drained off specie to the North
in payment for food. Louisiana, on the other hand, was
able to exchange sugar and molasses.[3] These railroad and
improvement banks passed out of existence in the depression period and a new organization was created. This was
the Union Bank of Mississippi.

In contrast to the reform movement in Louisiana, Mississippi sought relief by chartering the giant Union Bank of
1838. With an optimism unchastened by experience, this
bank was projected with an authorized tax-exempt capital

1861, 1866, and 1871. *Tenth Census* (VII), 'A History of State Debts,'
pp. 595–97.

[1] 24th Cong., 2d Sess., *House Ex. Doc.* No. 65, pp. 156–57.

[2] 24th Cong., 2d Sess., *House Ex. Doc.* No. 65, pp. 156–57. By this
report of 1837 ten banks and ten branches are listed. By the report of
the bank commissioners January 12, 1838, the total number of banks
and branches are twenty-eight. The ratio of specie, one to fifteen, is a
generous one, since the commissioners examined but seventeen banks,
the others insisting that no authority existed for an examination. In the
case of one railroad bank the specie ratio was one to thirty-four. *Senate
Journal*, 1838, pp. 120–32.

[3] *Senate Journal*, 1838, p. 130.

of $15,500,000, to be obtained 'by means of a loan.' The capital was to be raised by a State bond issue which was to be delivered to the bank and sold in Europe or the East. Stockholders were required to be citizens of Mississippi and could not transfer their shares to any person other than a citizen, until after five years. Stockholders paid in two and one half per cent of their subscription in money which was to be refunded to them after the organization began operations. The stock for which they subscribed was in reality paid for by real estate mortgages. These mortgages were to be on 'cultivated lands, plantations and slaves, town lots with houses'; but mortgages on other property yielding rent, uncultivated land 'susceptible of being cultivated,' and unimproved lots were also permitted. Two thirds of all loans were to be made on mortgages and payable on an eight-year amortization plan. The remaining one third of the loans were to be made on promissory notes and bills of exchange. The parent bank was located at Jackson, the State was divided into districts with a branch in each, and loans were to be distributed over the State.[1] A 'supplemental act,' passed ten days later, required the Governor to subscribe for stock on behalf of the State to an amount of fifty thousand shares of the original capital, to be paid for from the proceeds of bonds authorized by the original charter. Profits from the State's shares were devoted to 'internal improvements and the promotion of education.'[2] This supplemental act later became a vital point in the argument for repudiation. The State Constitution since 1832 prescribed a very rigid process for the pledge of State faith. Any such act must pass one legislature, be referred to the next succeeding body, and in the meantime be published in three newspapers

[1] *Laws*, 1838, pp. 9–33, February 5, 1838.

[2] *Ibid.*, 1838, pp. 33–44, February 15, 1838. In the Senate, during consideration of this act, Tucker, later repudiating Governor, moved an amendment requiring the law to pass by the process prescribed in the Constitution. The motion, however, was rejected by a vote of 21 to 3. (*Senate Journal*, 1838, p. 312; *Democratic Review*, X, p. 5.) This may mean either that a group questioned the legality of the proceeding from the outset, or that the attention of the Legislature being specifically drawn to the matter saw no point in the objection. Governor McNutt, who later stressed the point, did not veto the act.

three months preceding the election. If the newly elected legislature confirmed the act, it was then law.[1] The original charter passed strictly in accordance with this process; first in 1837, again in 1838, and was signed by Governor Alexander G. McNutt on February 5, 1838.[2] The supplemental act, however, did not pass by this process.

Since the bonds issued under these acts became the center of controversy and repudiation, it is necessary to state the facts sharply. In the period of June 5–9, 1838, Governor McNutt signed and delivered to the Union Bank for State stock six per cent bonds, amounting to $5,000,000. These consisted of 625 bonds due February 5, 1850, and 1875 bonds due February 5, 1858, all of a par value of $2000.[3] They were to draw interest at six per cent from date of issue, payable

[1] Thorpe, IV, p. 2061.

[2] Josiah A. P. Campbell, 'Planters and Union Bank Bonds.' Mississippi Historical Society *Publications*, IV (1905), p. 496. The author, a prominent member of the Mississippi bench and bar, writes: 'The 5th section of this act providing for the issue of bonds, and pledging the faith of the State... was passed as required by the Constitution....'

[3] 26th Cong., 1st Sess., *House Ex. Doc.* No. 172, pp. 472; 561–64; *Power of Attorney to Commissioners to sell State Bonds*, issued by H. G. Runnels, President of the Union Bank, June, 1838. These bonds were issued in two groups of five series each as follows:

TWELVE-YEAR BONDS

Date of Issue	Due Date	No. of Bonds	Serial Numbers
June 5, 1838	Feb. 5, 1850	125	1–125
June 6, 1838	Feb. 5, 1850	125	126–250
June 7, 1838	Feb. 5, 1850	125	251–375
June 8, 1838	Feb. 5, 1850	125	376–500
June 9, 1838	Feb. 5, 1850	125	501–625
Totals		625	or $1,250,000

TWENTY-YEAR BONDS

Date of Issue	Due Date	No. of Bonds	Serial Numbers
June 5, 1838	Feb. 5, 1858	375	1– 375
June 6, 1838	Feb. 5, 1858	375	376– 750
June 7, 1838	Feb. 5, 1858	375	751–1125
June 8, 1838	Feb. 5, 1858	375	1126–1500
June 9, 1838	Feb. 5, 1858	375	1501–1875
Totals		1875	or $3,750,000
Grand Total		2500	or $5,000,000

semi-annually, September 1 and March 1. Three commissioners, James C. Wilkins, William M. Pinckard, and Edward C. Wilkinson, were appointed to negotiate the sale, and instructed to urge the arguments that Mississippi was the largest cotton-producing State, and that the bonds were secured by a pledge of State faith made after an unusually rigid process.[1] The commissioners proceeded to Philadelphia in July, entered negotiations with Nicholas Biddle, and closed the contract on August 18, 1838. By the terms of this contract, the principal and interest were made payable in London at a rate of four shillings sixpence per dollar. The purchase money was to be paid by Biddle to the Union Bank in 'lawful money of the United States' in five installments of $1,000,000 each; on November 1, 1838, and January 1, March 1, May 1, and July 1, 1839. The United States Bank of Pennsylvania at Philadelphia guaranteed the contract. Biddle subsequently disposed of the larger part of these bonds to London and Dutch brokers.[2] In the summer of 1839, Governor McNutt delivered to the bank a second block of bonds, amounting to $5,000,000; and, although President Runnels himself went East in an effort to sell them, he was unable to do so. On November 18, 1839, the bank suggested to McNutt that he sign and deliver the remaining $5,500,000; but he refused to do so, and in a message to the Legislature January 4, 1840, he requested the recall of the second group. On March 2, 1840, by public proclamation, he warned all prospective buyers of the unsold bonds that in case they bought them below par, the State would not recognize them.[3] This prevented the sale of the second group, and the question thereafter was upon the legality of the first group already issued and in the hands of the Dutch and English investors.

In the meantime, the Governor and bank commissioners, created under an act of May 12, 1837, were at odds with the Union Bank. By a letter of November 23, 1838, President Runnels notified the commissioners that their 'application to examine the bank is simply but decidedly refused, and

[1] 26th Cong., 1st Sess., *House Ex. Doc.* No. 172, pp. 564–66.

[2] *Ibid.*, pp. 567–68.

[3] *Ibid.*, pp. 605; 691.

the correspondence closed.' The bank preferred to be inspected by the Legislature, as provided by its charter, rather than by a commission with 'preconceived opinions.'[1] Governor McNutt's message, January 8, 1839, reflected a growing irritation. He was not opposed to banks if prudently conducted, but, he thought, 'it cannot be denied... that moneyed associations of wealth are anti-republican in their tendency; and, when perverted to the purposes of speculation, have a withering influence, both on the planting and commercial interest.' Many of them were tax-exempt, arrogantly resisted public inspection, engaged in cotton speculation, and flooded the State with an inflated currency, the continual expansion and contraction of which amounted to a direct tax upon the population. He proposed a general banking law of strict provisions to which all must conform under penalty of forfeiture of charters. He suggested that they be required to keep a specie reserve equal to one third of their circulation. The New York system, however, under the existing circumstances would only aggravate the distress. He called attention to the $7,000,000 of bonds issued; and judged it highly important 'that the interest be punctually paid... and ample funds provided for the redemption of the principal.' He concluded, however, that it was 'usually much easier to borrow and spend money than to provide the means of payment.' There was no recommendation for repudiation in this message; although the argument later used was here stated. It was his opinion that the bank had violated its charter, for the money from Biddle would not all be delivered until July 1, 1839. Interest, however, was being paid on the total bond issue from June, 1838.[2] It is clear that McNutt was in an anti-bank mood that promised to be a spur to reform had it not pushed him into repudiation as the distress deepened. He had made some of the most valuable reform suggestions of the period, and his anti-bank attitude was no more violent than that of scores of other persons in the West at the same time.

A joint legislative committee of ten members investigated the bank in January, 1839. A majority of eight agreed upon

[1] 26th Cong., 1st Sess., *House Ex. Doc.* No. 172, p. 479.
[2] *Ibid.*, pp. 451–75, January 8, 1839.

a report, Tucker and Foote, later governors, dissenting. The bank officials, said the majority report, were entirely justified in refusing to submit to an examination by the bank commissioners. The bank had manifested toward the committee 'a frank, open, and unhesitating' disposition to assist the investigation; and an examination of the books showed a 'painful anxiety to pursue the charter to the letter.' The Biddle negotiation had been 'highly advantageous to the State and the Bank, and in accordance with the injunctions of the charter....' Post-notes, indeed, had been issued, redeemable August 1, 1839; but with banks in suspension elsewhere, regular circulation payable on demand was impossible, and these post-notes had afforded sorely needed credit. Discounts had begun September 27, 1838, and were well distributed, the average loan being $1800. Two cases of $10,000 loans to private persons and two cases of $15,000 loans to directors were noted. The charges regarding cotton speculation were exaggerated. The bank had advanced money to planters on the crop of 1838, and had taken charge of its marketing; but there was no speculation in this. The motive had been to assist the movement of the crop, and prevent large commission charges at New Orleans. Its failure to extend its branches for interior loans was due to the distress of the times.[1] Henry S. Foote, in a minority report, was less favorable and distinctly satirical. The committee had been received by the bank officials 'in a manner entirely satisfactory'; but he observed nothing in that manner to provoke such enthusiastic encomium. There was no evidence of '*corruption*,' but much of a lack of '*authority* and *expediency*.' The charter had been violated by issuing post-notes instead of notes payable on demand, by cotton speculation, by refusal to establish branches, and by selling State bonds below par. He conceded, however, that the sale had been the best that could have been made in America.[2] A year later, McNutt declared to the Legislature that there had been 'culpable mismanagement and selfish favoritism'; that he had refused to execute the

[1] 26th Cong., 1st Sess., *House Ex. Doc.* No. 172, pp. 554-60, January 24, 1839.
[2] *Ibid.*, pp. 568-89.

remaining bonds; but there was still no suggestion of repudiation.[1]

REPUDIATION MOVEMENT

On January 5, 1841, however, Governor McNutt definitely advised repudiation of the Union Bank bonds. He declared that there was no prospect that either the Planters or the Union Bank could pay the principal of the bonds at maturity, or the interest payments accruing in the year 1841. The banking system of the State was vicious and it could never be so regulated as to become useful to any community. He alleged as reasons why the Union Bank bonds should be repudiated; that the United States Bank of Pennsylvania, by acting as a guarantee for Biddle's purchase, had violated a provision of its own charter prohibiting it from dealing in State securities; that the supplemental act of February 15, 1838, not having been confirmed by a subsequent legislature, was unconstitutional; and that the bank had sold the bonds below par, since interest to an amount of about $170,000 had accrued upon the bonds before the purchase money had been delivered by Biddle. Furthermore, the Eleventh Amendment of the United States Constitution would protect the State from any suit in the Supreme Court.[2] In addition to $125,000 of the Planters' Bank bond principal, due July 1, 1841, there came due the semi-annual interest payments on the bonds; all of which went delinquent in the year 1841.[3] By deed of assign-

[1] 26th Cong., 1st Sess., *House Ex.* Doc. No. 172. p. 605, January 14, 1840.

[2] 22d Cong., 2d Sess., *House Ex. Doc.* No. 111, pp. 1098–1102, January 5, 1841.

[3] 29th Cong., 1st Sess., *House Ex. Doc.* No. 226, pp. 859–61. The Planters' Bank bonds are described in the following table:

ISSUE OF 1831

Date of Issue	Due Date	No. of Bonds	Serial Numbers
July 1, 1831	July 1, 1841	125	1–125
July 1, 1831	July 1, 1846	125	126–250
July 1, 1831	July 1, 1851	125	251–375
July 1, 1831	July 1, 1856	125	376–500
Totals..................................... 500		or	$500,000

ment the Union Bank went into liquidation on October 29, 1841.[1] Governor McNutt, however, was unable to carry the repudiation proposal in 1841. The Legislature resolved that the State was bound for both principal and interest, and should 'pay her bonds and preserve her faith inviolate';[2] and the Attorney-General, in an opinion July 7, 1841, held the State liable.[3]

Throughout the year 1841 many letters came to Governor McNutt from bondholders. These he communicated to the Legislature under the caption: *Letters from Fundmongers.* Seventeen London bondholders, joining in a letter of May 1, called attention to the great resources of the State as a cotton-producing center and the damage 'which the irregularity must do to all the sister States of the Union.' R. W. Morrison, Sons and Company, of London, stated that this delinquency would not only 'injure most seriously... the credit of your State, but... prejudice generally the credit of all the States in the Union.' Mr. John James Rorie, of Plymouth, England, wrote that he held two bonds purchased at 112½, which was certainly above '*par*,' and that the present quotation was 75, '*although not saleable.*' Letters from James B. Murray, of New York, and Hope and Company, of Amsterdam, were of the same general tenor.[4]

ISSUE OF 1833

Date of Issue	Due Date	No. of Bonds	Serial Numbers
March 1, 1833	March 1, 1861	500	501–1000
March 1, 1833	March 1, 1866	500	1001–1500
March 1, 1833	March 1, 1871	500	1501–2000
Totals................................... 1500 or $1,500,000			

The semi-annual interest payments on these bonds became due January 1, March 1, July 1, September 1, 1841. The *Bankers' Magazine* listed these bonds as delinquent since July 1 and September 1, 1840. It appears also that some $88,000 in principal had been retired. (*Bankers' Magazine*, VII, p. 497.)

[1] *Senate Journal*, 1842, pp. 90–99.

[2] *Bankers' Magazine*, VII, p. 423.

[3] Hazards, *United States Commercial and Statistical Register*, V, pp. 128–34.

[4] 29th Cong., 1st Sess., *House Ex. Doc.* No. 226, pp. 856–64. To Hope and Company, of Amsterdam, which held a large number of these Union

The question of repudiating the Union Bank bonds was a primary issue in the State election of November, 1841, with Tucker, the Democratic candidate for Governor, favoring repudiation; and Shattuck, the Whig candidate, favoring payment. The election supported repudiation by seating Tucker and a Democratic Legislature.[1] Governor McNutt's message of January 4, 1842, renewed his demand for repudiation, declaring that the election had 'gloriously sustained the sacred truth that the toiling millions never should be burdened with taxes for the idle few.' A committee report to the lower house presented by James E. Mathews, and a report of a joint committee presented by Upton Miller and H. W. Flournoy, supported this view, comparing themselves to the Patriots of the American and French Revolutions. The formal act of repudiation was enacted February 21, 1842.[2] The question of State liability for the Union Bank bonds came before the High Court of Errors and Appeals, which in April, 1853, held, in an elaborate argument, that the State was liable.[3] Neither the principal nor the interest since 1841, however, has been paid. By an amendment to the Constitution of 1876, continued in the Constitution of 1890, the Legislature is denied power to pay the bonds.[4]

The action in 1842 related to the Union Bank bonds and did not include the $2,000,000 of Planters' Bank bonds, the validity of which was recognized by Governors Tucker and Brown.[5] In 1852, however, the direct question was put to

Bank bonds, Governor McNutt in a letter of May 22, 1841, estimates the State's loss at a much higher figure than in his message of January, 1841. In a carefully itemized statement he computes the loss of interest from June 6, 1838, to July 1, 1839, plus the loss in difference between 'current money of the United States' and English sterling at four shillings six-pence at $1,084,781.30.

[1] Brough, pp. 335–36.

[2] 29th Cong., 1st Sess., *House Ex. Doc.* No. 226, pp. 851–56; 876; 882–83.

[3] *State of Mississippi v. Hezron Johnson* (April, 1853), in 25 Miss., pp. 625–880.

[4] Thorpe, IV, pp. 2089; 2125.

[5] *Speeches, Messages and Writings of Albert Gallatin Brown* (Philadelphia, 1859), pp. 53; 77; 88; 93.

the voters of the State: 'Will you submit to a direct tax, for the purpose of paying the Planters' Bank bonds?' The result of the election was against payment,[1] and the constitutional prohibition against payment of these bonds is included in the Constitutions of 1876 and 1890. After the collapse of Mississippi banks in the forties, regular issue banking virtually ceased to exist in the State prior to the Civil War. As late as January, 1860, only one small institution was reported — the Northern Bank at Holly Springs.[2]

The argument against the legality of the Union Bank bonds cannot be accepted as tenable, and possesses no merit, except a strained technicality. It is obviously a rationalization of the deeper reason of debtor distress, similar to that which in the West of the forties drove the paper money banker from the frontier, and in the West after the Civil War stood ready to scale debts by greenbacks and free silver. In the first place, the charter of the Union Bank, admitted legal by all parties, clearly authorized a $15,500,-000 bond issue pledged by State faith. The supplemental act of February 15, 1838, added nothing to the total liability of the State. It merely required the Governor to use $5,000,-000 of the bonds already authorized to purchase on behalf of the State fifty thousand shares of bank stock. True, it required a State investment; whereas the charter merely provided for State aid. That, however, is a distinction without a difference. Regarding the claim that the Union Bank and not the State received the money, it must be said that this argument and that regarding the supplemental act are mutually destructive. If the bonds were issued, as claimed, under the supplemental act, the State would appear to have received the money to purchase shares; but if the bonds were not issued under the supplemental act, they were issued under the charter. That they were issued under the charter, however, would seem to be established by the

---

[1] 29th Cong., 1st Sess., *House Ex. Doc.* No. 226, pp. 887–88; 894. *Bankers' Magazine*, VII, pp. 492; 499. It appears that any voter of the State failing to vote in this election was counted in favor of payment, but the majority against payment as computed by the *Vicksburg Whig* was something over 4000 more than the silent vote and the positive vote.

[2] 34th Cong., 3d Sess., *House Ex. Doc.* No. 87, p. 150.

fact that they were to come due twelve and twenty years from February 5, 1838, the date of the final enactment of the charter. The case against legality is further weakened by the fact that the repudiation argument was not seriously urged until the failure of the bank was imminent; although Governor McNutt had stated in January, 1839, that the process was irregular, and Tucker, in the Senate, had objected to the act of February 5, 1838. Regarding the claim that the bonds were sold below par, it must be conceded that Biddle drove a close bargain; but it is difficult to see any more than that. Finally, the highest court of the State, in 1853, held the State liable; and there can be no doubt that, had the Supreme Court of the United States possessed jurisdiction, it would have held likewise. Barred by the Eleventh Amendment from a suit in the Supreme Court, bondholders have been unable to carry the matter further, and neither interest nor principal has been paid since 1841.

LATER HISTORY OF REPUDIATED DEBTS

Although the debt was not paid, it subsequently rose at times to National attention. On the eve of the Civil War the Planters' Bank bondholders petitioned the Legislature to make some arrangement for settlement. Governor William McWillie communicated this to the Legislature with a favorable recommendation, and a minority committee report favored payment. A joint committee in February, 1860, however, returned a majority report against any agitation of a subject which might divide the people 'in view of the present aspect of political affairs.' [1]

During the Civil War the matter assumed primary importance. The Confederacy hoped to negotiate loans in England, and it became the business of Robert J. Walker to defeat this. He had migrated to Mississippi from Pennsylvania and had risen to public prominence as Secretary of the Treasury under Polk and as Governor of the Territory of Kansas under Buchanan. As Secretary of the Treasury, he had caused to be collected in 1846 the most elaborate reports on State banking made during the period, and was

[1] *Bankers' Magazine*, XIV, pp. 509–11; 861–67.

thoroughly familiar with the repudiation movement. Upon
the outbreak of the Civil War, he offered his services to the
Union, and by the testimony of Chase became an early
advocate of a National Banking System. At a critical
moment he was sent to London as a confidential agent to
destroy the credit of the Confederacy. By personal influence and pamphlets he accomplished his object. His argument in London was naturally clever diplomacy rather than
critical history. At any rate, it was effective and, in view
of the Fourteenth Amendment, was sound financial advice.
He did not neglect the opportunity to point out that the
repudiated debts had been contracted by the seceded States
of Florida, Arkansas, and Mississippi; and that Jefferson
Davis, President of the Confederacy, came from Mississippi
and had published letters in 1849 which appeared to defend
the course of the State.[1]

[1] Robert J. Walker, *American Slavery and Finances* (London, 1864).
From a purely historical standpoint, however, Walker, no doubt, misrepresented the facts; that is, if he meant to say that Davis was active in
the repudiation movement of 1842. A careful study of the relation of
Davis to this movement has led the author to the following conclusions:
(1) Davis, not entering Mississippi politics until 1843, could, obviously,
have had no connection with the movement in 1842; (2) he at no time
questioned the legality of the Planters' Bank bonds; (3) he regarded the
Union Bank bonds as illegally issued and, therefore, constituted no
obligation on the State. He defended the act of 1842, however, with
arguments similar to those used by McNutt. He held, however, that
the debt was one in equity and made efforts to secure its discharge by
voluntary subscription. Although believing it an illegal bond issue, he
expressed willingness to try the question before the courts. He appeared,
moreover, to be at odds with the Democratic repudiators who nominated
him as a candidate for the Legislature in 1843. A debate on the question
between him and S. S. Prentiss was scheduled to take place at Vicksburg
during the election. This did not occur on the date set, November 4,
1843, the reason being, according to the *Vicksburg Whig*, that Davis
'declined making a speech, stating that his party declared they would
not attend the meeting.' The *Whig* declared that the repudiators had
been unfortunate in selecting their candidate — that they 'had set up
a claim to decency by nominating Mr. Davis....' Davis later declared
that the active repudiators fought him in 1845 when he ran for Congress,
and always insisted that Walker misrepresented him — referring to him
as 'that lying emissary to England.' Professor W. E. Dodd, the closest
student of Walker and Davis, thinks Walker knew all the while the real
attitude of Davis. The view of Davis was much like that of such a good
lawyer as Benjamin R. Curtis, who wrote in 1844 on the legal aspect,

At the close of Reconstruction, the people of Mississippi were in no mood to make a distinction between either the Planters' Bank bonds, the Union Bank bonds, or Reconstruction bonds. By a constitutional amendment, adopted in 1875 by a large majority, the Legislature was forbidden to pay the bonds — a provision which was continued in the present Constitution of 1890.[1] In 1878, English bondholders, represented by Edward Hazelwood, of London, proposed a compromise by which certain public lands were to be taken in payment. The majority report of a committee of the Legislature on this proposal pleaded lack of jurisdiction, citing the amendment to the Constitution ratified November 2, 1875, by a vote of 128,648 to 26,987. A minority report, presented by Charles H. Wood, insisted on payment, citing court decisions which recognized State liability.[2]

This subject must not be dismissed, however, without noting that State delinquency was not limited to Mississippi. The London *Times* in 1860 listed six States as either repudiating or delinquent; namely, Mississippi, Arkansas, Florida, Michigan, Indiana, and Pennsylvania.[3] The State

apart from the Eleventh Amendment: 'The State of Mississippi would not be legally bound to pay the debt.' (*Life and Writings of Benjamin R. Curtis*, II, pp. 93 ff.) This was written in 1844, however, when Curtis was a relatively young man and was an answer to European reflections on American financial honor. It must be estimated with the same indulgence as the letter of Davis in 1849 defending his State against what he regarded as a 'savage attack.' Theodore Roosevelt went far out of his way to make an historical error in his *Life of Benton*, p. 220. His reference to Davis as 'chief repudiator' was a greater error than that of Walker, since Walker was engaged on a diplomatic rather than an historical task. Excerpts from the files of the *Vicksburg Whig* have been supplied by the Honorable W. M. Drake, of Church Hill, Mississippi, who has manifested a lively interest in the matter and who has recently been in correspondence with English bondholders, offering to pay some of the bonds from his private fortune. Two letters by Davis written in 1875 are in Rowland, *Jefferson Davis*, III, pp. 453; 474. The letter defending the State in 1849 is not in the Rowland collection. It may be found in *Bankers' Magazine*, IV, pp. 363–70.

[1] Thorpe, IV, 2089; 2125.

[2] Mississippi *House Journal* (1880), pp. 264; 601–03.

[3] *Bankers' Magazine*, XIV, p. 63. The repudiation movement in general is ably presented in W. A. Scott, *Repudiation of State Debts* (New York, 1893). The *ante-bellum* repudiation in Arkansas and Florida is

of Pennsylvania had borrowed in Europe more heavily than any State, and her delinquency naturally attracted more attention. It became the butt of the caustic wit of Sidney Smith, of Saint Paul's,[1] the gibe of London doggerel verse,[2] and the subject of a biting sonnet by William Wordsworth.[3] In more recent times the matter of repudiation has emerged into prominence again — embarrassing the various movements toward international association and the funding of the World War debts.[4]

discussed elsewhere in this study. State delinquency became so general as to affect the National credit, the Government being unable to float a loan in Europe in 1842. Moreover, a movement got under way for federal assumption, but failed to materialize. (Benton, *Thirty Years' View*, II, pp. 171–76; 240–47; 467.)

[1] E. A. Duyckinck, *The Wit and Wisdom of the Reverend Sidney Smith.* Sidney Smith, of Saint Paul's, had invested some money in Pennsylvania bonds and the interest being delinquent, wrote his cutting remarks in a direct petition to the Legislature of Pennsylvania. His bomb, he thought, had been successful and the list of casualties extensive, for he had received many letters calling him a thief, monster, and deist. Duff Green, indeed, had sent his respects with three pounds of cheese. To Captain Morgan, of the Atlantic liner, Southhampton, Smith wrote: ' My opinion is... that Pennsylvania will *not* pay.'

[2] *Ibid.*, pp. 70–71. A parody made its way about London, two verses of which follow:

Yankee Doodle borrows cash,
Yankee Doodle spends it
And then he snaps his fingers at
The jolly flat who lends it.
Ask him when he means to pay
He shows no hesitation,
But says he'll take the shortest way
And that's Repudiation.

Great and free Amerikee
With all the world is vying.
That she the '*land of promise*' is
There's surely no denying.
But be it known henceforth to all
Who hold their I.O.U.'s, sirs,
A Yankee Doodle *promise* is
A Yankee *Doodle do*, sirs.

[3] Thomas Hutchinson (editor), *Wordsworth's Poetical Works* (London, 1926), p. 515. See Sonnet, entitled 'To the Pennsylvanians,' reading:

All who revere the memory of Penn
Grieve for the land on whose wild woods his name
Was fondly grafted with a virtuous aim,
Renounced, abandoned by degenerate men
For State-dishonour black as ever came
To upper air from Mammon's loathsome den.

[4] On the more recent aspects of the matter see: C. P. Holland, 'Our Repudiated State Debts,' in *Foreign Affairs*, VI (1928), pp. 395–407; R. M. Borchel, 'Repudiation — A Senatorial Nightmare,' in *Independ-*

FLUSH TIMES IN ALABAMA

The Alabama Constitution of 1819 empowered the Legislature to create a State bank, and other banks and branches, provided that each reserved to the State at least two fifths of its capital stock.[1] In 1819, there were already three banks operating under Territorial charters: the Merchants' and Planters' Bank of Huntsville, created by Mississippi Territory in 1816 before the separation, the Tombeckbee Bank of St. Stephens, and the Bank of Mobile — the latter two created by Alabama Territory in the years 1818 and 1819 respectively. Only the Bank of Mobile survived the panic of 1819. The State shortly thereafter established the Bank of the State, located first at Cahawba, but later removed to Tuscaloosa. In this the State invested various funds, derived from federal land donations for education, for a seat of government, and the three per cent fund from land sales. In addition, State bonds were issued from time to time.[2] Alabama, caught in the grip of the speculative forces of the thirties, reacted no less violently than did Mississippi or Michigan. Her method, however, was the inflation of the existing organizations rather than a wholesale creation of new ones.[3] Between 1823 and 1837, something over $15,500,-

---

ent, CVII (1926), pp. 73–75; and Mark Sullivan, 'Present Status of Repudiated State Bonds,' in *North American Review*, CLXX (1900), pp. 480–92.

[1] Thorpe, I, p. 111. This constitution shows the spur of anti-bank feeling engendered by the panic of 1819, in that charters must pass by two thirds vote, each session of the Legislature was limited to one charter, stockholders were liable to the amount of their shares, and each organization was required to have a minimum of $100,000 capital, fifty per cent paid in specie before the beginning of business.

[2] *Tenth Census*, VII, p. 590; Thomas Perkins Abernethy, 'Formative Period in Alabama,' Alabama State Department of Archives and History *Publications* (1922), pp. 93–101.

[3] Charles A. Conant, *History of Modern Banks of Issue* (New York, 1896), pp. 333–34. The inflation is thus described: 'Candidates for General Assembly were compelled to promise their supporters liberal loans in case of election, and to exact pledges from candidates for directorships that the loans would be granted. One of the hotel-keepers of Tuscaloosa succeeded in securing election as director in 1832 and the hotel swarmed with members of the Legislature and persons desiring to borrow money... four of the hotel-keepers realized that they were con-

ooo in bonds were authorized, the inflation growing as the panic neared.[1] Not all bonds authorized were issued, however, but the total amount issued was in excess of that of Mississippi.[2] So great was the enthusiasm for banks that by an act of January 9, 1836, direct taxation was virtually abolished and the sum of $100,000 (dividends expected from State bank stock) was devoted to pay State expenses.[3]

By 1837, three banks and four branches were in operation. These consisted of the Bank of the State at Tuscaloosa, with four branches at Mobile, Montgomery, Decauter, and Huntsville; the Planters' and Merchants' Bank of Mobile; and the Bank of Mobile.[4] Mobile, by virtue of its great commercial importance, naturally had the largest concentration of bank capital. The largest bank in the State Bank system and two large independent organizations were located there. Moreover, about fifty-five per cent of the total bank capital of the State was at Mobile. 'Cotton,' said the officials of the State Bank in June, 1837, 'is the basis of the entire operations of this place; it pervades the business of every man.'[5] From January 1, 1835, to May 1, 1837, the average ratio of specie to liability for the State Bank and its branches was 1 to 7.11;[6] and for all the banks of the State on June 1, 1837, the ratio was about 1 to 12.[7] These figures clearly reveal the extreme frailty of the

ducting their business under a heavy handicap and secured their own election as directors in 1834....'

[1] *Tenth Census*, VII, pp. 590–92; Trotter, pp. 322–32. The following is a table of bonds authorized for the Bank of the State in addition to some $600,000 issued for the Bank of Mobile:

Date of Issue	Amount
1823	$ 100,000
1828	100,000
1832	1,300,000
1833	3,500,000
1836	2,400,000
1837	7,500,000
	$14,900,000

[2] 29th Cong., 1st Sess., *House Ex. Doc.* No. 226, pp. 802–04. By 1844 the actual State debt due to the bond issues was $9,215,055.

[3] *Tenth Census*, VII, p. 592.

[4] 24th Cong., 2d Sess., *House Ex. Doc.* No. 65, pp. 146–47.

[5] 25th Cong., 2d Sess., *House Ex. Doc.* No. 79, pp. 519; 510–13.

[6] *Ibid.*, 3d Sess., *House Ex. Doc.* No. 227, p. 471.

[7] *Ibid.*, 2d Sess., *House Ex. Doc.* No. 79, p. 519.

system — large circulation and deposit liability with a small specie reserve, and loans which could not be collected without a tedious process of foreclosure which county officials refused to enforce. Depositors and billholders demanded specie which the banks did not have. Attempting to move the cotton crop in order to bring specie from Liverpool, they advanced to planters, which only involved them deeper, for the cotton market fell, and planters were unable to meet either their advances or previous loans.[1]

In an attempt to relieve debtors from collection pressure, the Legislature passed a relief act which authorized additional loans and the repayment of old loans in three annual installments. At that time bad debts were estimated at five per cent of the total; but these increased to seventeen per cent in 1840, and after a second relief act rose to thirty per cent by 1844. From these circumstances it was obvious that the banks were insolvent, and that the bonds issued and the educational funds invested were State liabilities. The Legislature, therefore, repealed the charters of the four branches of the State Bank and allowed the parent bank at Tuscaloosa to expire by limitation on January 4, 1844. All these were placed in liquidation, and Governor J. L. Martin opposed any further stay laws, demanding immediate action against debtors to force whatever collection was possible. By 1844, the total liability of the State from its banking venture was in excess of $14,000,000, consisting of over $9,000,000 for bonds issued, $3,000,000 for circulation, and the remainder for university and school funds. The annual interest charge was estimated at more than four times the cost of the State Government, and it was thought that not more than one half of the debt could be paid from final liquidation. This huge debt, in a State which some years before had abolished taxation, was a staggering burden; yet there was little serious talk of repudiation. Efforts were immediately made to meet the debt by taxation.[2]

In response to the recommendation of Governor Martin, a law was passed February 4, 1846, to regulate the affairs of

[1] 25th Cong., 2d Sess., *House Ex. Doc.* No. 79, pp. 510–13.

[2] 29th Cong., 1st Sess., *House Ex. Doc.* No. 226, pp. 802–25; 26th Cong., 2d Sess., *House Ex. Doc.* No. 111, pp. 542–48.

the bank and provide for the payment of State bonds. This arranged for commissioners to take control of the bank and its branches, collect loans, pay interest on the bonds, and redeem the circulation.[1] This liquidation process, however, was a tedious one, and the affairs of these old banks were not completely settled until after the panic of 1857.[2]

After the distress of the forties, banking in Alabama never attained the popularity which it enjoyed in the thirties. The old Bank of Mobile continued in operation, joined by some seven small institutions at various points in the State in the fifties. The entire circulation and deposits of all the Alabama banks on January 1, 1861, was little more than that of the old Mobile branch of the State Bank in 1837. Loans were smaller but the specie reserve was over twenty times as large.[3] Alabama, with a larger liability from her banking ventures, escaped the repudiation which overtook her sister State of Mississippi.

THE FLORIDA BOOM

Although Florida could boast of the oldest settlement in America at St. Augustine, its first real development did not come until after its cession to the United States. In the expansion period of the Jacksonian era, the rich lands of upper and West Florida drew the Territory into the maelstrom of the plantation movement.

By 1837, the Legislative Council had incorporated nine banks and authorized for their aid a bond issue of over $9,000,000.[4] The Union Bank, the largest of these, was a typical land bank of the Cotton Belt. By 1835, $1,000,000 in bonds had been delivered to it, and it began business on

---

[1] 30th Cong., 1st Sess., *House Ex. Doc.* No. 77, pp. 491–501, Commissioners Report of December 20, 1847.

[2] 35th Cong., 1st Sess., *House Ex. Doc.* No 107, pp. 195–96.

[3] This paragraph is based on reports in *House Executive Documents* from the 30th to the 36th Congress.

[4] 24th Cong., 2d Sess., *House Ex. Doc.* No. 65, pp. 144–45. These had been created since 1829, the Union Bank in 1833. Secondary accounts will be found in William Watson Davis, 'Civil War and Reconstruction in Florida,' Columbia University *Studies*, LIII (1913), pp. 22–28; and David Y. Thomas, 'Banking in the Territory of Florida,' *South Atlantic Quarterly*, IX (1910), pp. 251–66.

January 16, 1835. Its report at the close of the first year showed that it was extending large loans on the security of its own stock. This system of capitalization by a bond issue secured by mortgages, of stock subscription paid for by further mortgages, and loans secured by stock, brought a heavy demand for stock. But all could not invest, however, for the greater amount of the stock was allotted to eighty-eight out of four hundred and four applicants. The Governor delivered a second block of bonds to the bank amounting to $2,000,000, and the proceeds were employed in the same manner as the first series.[1] The coming of the panic toppled this pyramid of finance into ruins. Land values depreciated, and mortgages deposited as security for bonds and in payment of shares depreciated in proportion. The bank could neither pay its depositors, collect its loans, nor redeem its circulation; and the mortgages, even after a tedious process of foreclosure, could be expected to yield little except anti-bank feeling and political reprisal. To render matters worse, part of the proceeds of the second bond issue was used to pay interest on the first. The banks failed to meet interest payments, and the burden of the debt fell on the Territory. This debt, including bond issues for two other banks, amounted to $3,900,000.[2]

The delinquency was anticipated and the repudiation sentiment was strong. A committee of the Legislature on February 25, 1840, reported that $3,900,000 in bonds 'purporting to be guaranteed by the Territory' had already been issued, and that the banks were claiming $5,600,000 more under their charters. The annual interest charge was already $230,000 and would amount to $570,000 if the other bonds were issued. 'Indeed,' continued the report, 'such a sum could not be paid by taxation, but only by the absolute

[1] 26th Cong., 1st Sess., *House Ex. Doc.* No. 172, pp. 431–35, gives a general history from the beginning; and 26th Cong., 2d Sess., *House Ex. Doc.* No. 111, pp. 278–98, gives a detailed account of the bonds.

[2] 29th Cong., 1st Sess., *House Ex. Doc.* No. 226, p. 773, Message of Governor Call, January 5, 1843. Bonds had been issued as follows: Union Bank, $1,000,000 due in four installments in 1858, 1860, 1862, 1864; and $2,000,000 due in four installments in 1862, 1864, 1866, 1868. Southern Life Insurance and Trust Company, $4000,000 due in 1865. Bank of Pensacola $500,000 due in 1860. (Trotter, pp. 344–45.)

surrender of the property of our citizens.' The committee proceeded to argue that a Territory, not being sovereign, could not make a binding contract and its bonds were void. Moreover, it was argued that the Federal Government, since it had not exercised due supervision, should assume the burden. The question of legal liability was submitted to Chancellor Kent, Daniel Webster, Peter Jay, and Horace Binney. The opinion of all was that a Territory was competent to issue bonds and that its subsequent admission as a State could not impair the contract. Webster and Jay held, however, that Congress could set such contracts aside if it chose; although they thought such ought not to be done.[1] Another committee, reporting February 25, 1841, however, declared against 'the doctrine that this Territory is either competent or inclined to violate its plighted faith....'[2] In March, 1841, a popular referendum was held on the question of payment,[3] and the referendum favored repudiation, which was formally enacted in 1842.[4] Governor Call, an opponent of repudiation, had taken the attitude that European bondholders should first take action against the banks to force foreclosure on mortgages held as security for the bonds.[5] Governor Branch, however, in his message of January 10, 1845, upheld repudiation on the eve of statehood. 'She has been charged,' he declared, 'with repudiating her *just* debts.... On the contrary, it is anxiety to pay her *honest* debt that induces her to scrutinize the spurious demands of speculators and bank swindlers....'[6]

It was with this attitude that Florida entered the Union in 1845, denying the competency of a Territory to bind the State and the justice of the contract.[7] When Florida entered the Union, she had a constitution that was already six years old. The sobering effect of the Union Bank career is reflected in the debates and action of the convention which assembled

[1] 26th Cong., 2d Sess., *House Ex. Doc.* No. 111, pp. 257–78.

[2] 29th Cong., 2d Sess., *House Ex. Doc.* No. 227, p. 710.

[3] *Ibid.*, p. 734.   [4] Florida *Laws* (1842), p. 52.

[5] 29th Cong., 1st Sess., *House Ex. Doc.* No. 226, pp. 775–78; 735–48.

[6] *Ibid.*, pp. 779–82.

[7] *Florida Senate Journal* (1845), pp. 55–59, *Report of the Committee on Banks*, July 14, 1845.

at St. Joseph in 1838. Dominated by Jacksonian distrust of banks, and taught by bitter experience, it wrote into its constitution some of the most drastic and advanced banking clauses of the period. No bank official was eligible for State office, nor for one year after ceasing such duty. Before a charter could be granted, it must be given three months' publicity, pass by a two-thirds vote, and stockholders were made liable for debts to the amount of their shares. All banks were required to have a minimum of twenty stockholders, and charters were limited to twenty years without renewal. Each bank was required to have at least $100,000 paid in specie, and no loans were permitted on security of stock. Banks were forbidden to deal in real estate, stock, merchandise, chattels, insurance, manufacturing, export, import, or act as trustee for real estate. Total liability was limited to twice the capital, dividends were limited to ten per cent with all surplus carried to a safety-fund. Regular inspection and quarterly reports were required, and the State forbidden to pledge its faith for any bank liability. This constitution was submitted to the people and ratified January 11, 1839.[1] In a very real sense these bank articles reflect the history of Florida's early banking ventures. Although the constitution did not go into effect until 1845, it is surprising to note the advanced banking principles of this frontier community of fifty thousand population, acting under the anti-bank spur. In 1843, laws providing some of the most stringent regulations in the Union were passed. Directors were made liable to five years' imprisonment and a $5000 fine for failure to redeem, and stockholders were placed under triple liability, which was reduced to single liability in 1845.[2]

Although the new State refused to recognize either the debt or the existence of the banks, it was unable to prevent their operation. After 1845, however, they were little more than agencies of liquidation. By 1847, they had all expired except the Union Bank and the Southern Life whose bills

[1] 29th Cong., 1st Sess., *House Ex. Doc.* No. 226, pp. 731–32, text of bank articles.

[2] Davis R. Dewey, 'State Banking before the Civil War,' National Monetary Commission *Reports* (1910), p. 77.

were worth about twenty cents on the dollar.[1] The attitude of the new State toward the old banks is shown by the petulant tone of the following letter of the Secretary of State February 23, 1848: 'The fact is the authorities of this State have scrupulously avoided any communications with these institutions by which a recognition of their pretended charters... might be attributed to the authorities of this State.' Whenever officials of the State felt it necessary to refer to them, they used such expressions as: 'pretended,' 'alleged,' or 'claiming banking privileges.'[2] There were few banks thereafter before the Civil War. In 1859, two were organized: the State Bank of Florida at Tallahassee, and the Bank of St. Johns at Jacksonville. The combined circulation in 1860 was only $183,640, and deposits, $129,518.[3]

THE PORT OF THE GREAT VALLEY

With the exception of New York, the banking institutions of New Orleans were, perhaps, the most important of the Nation prior to the Civil War. Before the railroads and the war severed the economic ties, the Crescent City, as it liked to be called, was indeed the port of the Great Valley. As De Bow in the first issue of his *Review* compared the decline of his native city on the Ashley and the Cooper with the rising commercial importance of New Orleans — the shipping point for the sugar and cotton of the plantations, and the market for western farm and fur factory — it is not surprising that he was optimistic. If his dream of a new London on its Thames or a new Paris by its Seine showed an excess of exuberance, his statement that New Orleans was 'the great emporium of the South and West' was more nearly a sober fact.[4] The commerce of New Orleans being so varied, it is easy to see how her banks became involved in internal improvements, public utilities, and cotton and sugar planta-

[1] 29th Cong., 2d Sess., *House Ex. Doc.* No. 120, p. 207.

[2] 30th Cong., 1st Sess., *House Ex. Doc.* No. 77, p. 490, to the Secretary of Treasury.

[3] 36th Cong., 1st Sess., *House Ex. Doc.* No. 49, p. 161.

[4] *De Bow's Review*, I (1846), pp. 5; 44. According to tradition, the name 'Dixie' originated from the wide use in the South of the ten-dollar bank-notes of New Orleans with the French word 'Dix' printed on them.

tions. The panic drove home the lesson that banks must beware of such speculative involvements and content themselves with a lower but surer income. With the failure of the sugar and cotton market and the collapse of internal improvement ventures, the banks were confronted by an impossible situation. With a large circulation, inadequate reserves, and frozen assets, the system collapsed. Out of its ruins, however, emerged a reform movement that gave New Orleans a national reputation for sound banking and powerfully influenced the National System. These factors, therefore, entitle its banking history to careful consideration.

By 1837, the banks operating in Louisiana consisted of sixteen main organizations located at New Orleans and their thirty-one branches distributed over the State. All except three had been created since 1828. One of these operated the city waterworks, another the gasworks, and another ran a railroad. Two of the largest hotels of New Orleans were operated by banks.[1] For the assistance of five of these the State had issued in excess of $19,000,000 in bonds which had been sold in Europe.[2] Instead of the earlier practice, the

[1] 24th Cong., 2d Sess., *House Ex. Doc.* No. 65, pp. 148–51. The Improvement and Banking Company ran the St. Louis Hotel in the French quarter and the Exchange Bank ran the St. Charles Hotel in the American quarter. S. A. Trufant, ' Review of Banking in New Orleans, 1830–1840,' in Louisiana Historical Society *Proceedings and Reports* (1917), pp. 25–40.

[2] 25th Cong., 2d Sess., *House Ex. Doc.* No. 79, p. 670. Bonds had been issued as shown in the following table:

Name of Bank	Date of Issue	Purpose	Due	Amount	Where Held
Bank of Louisiana	July 1, 1824	State Shares	July 1, 1839	$600,000	Europe
Bank of Louisiana	July 1, 1824	State Shares	July 1, 1844	600,000	Europe
Bank of Louisiana	July 1, 1824	State Shares	July 1, 1849	600,000	Europe
Consolidated Ass'n.	Dec. 31, 1828	To Aid	June 30, 1838	171,000	Europe
Consolidated Ass'n.	Dec. 31, 1828	To Aid	June 30, 1843	833,000	Europe
Consolidated Ass'n.	May 1, 1836	To Aid	June 1, 1848	1,000,000	Europe
Mechanics and Traders	May 9, 1833	To Aid	May 9, 1853	150,000	Europe
Union Bank	Oct. 1, 1832	To Aid	Nov. 1, 1844	1,750,000	Europe
Union Bank	Oct. 1, 1832	To Aid	Nov. 1, 1847	1,750,000	Europe
Union Bank	Oct. 1, 1832	To Aid	Nov. 1, 1850	1,750,000	Europe
Union Bank	Oct. 1, 1832	To Aid	Nov. 1, 1852	1,750,000	Europe
Citizens Bank	Feb. 1, 1836	To Aid	Feb. 1, 1850	1,600,000	Europe
Citizens Bank	Feb. 1, 1836	To Aid	Feb. 1, 1859	1,600,000	Europe
Citizens Bank	Feb. 1, 1836	To Aid	Feb. 1, 1868	1,600,000	Europe
Citizens Bank	Feb. 1, 1836	To Aid	Feb. 1, 1877	1,600,000	Europe
Citizens Bank	Feb. 1, 1836	To Aid	Feb. 1, 1886	1,600,000	Europe

Total $19,204,000

State began the policy after 1828 of issuing bonds 'to aid,' a procedure like that of the Union Bank of Mississippi. Suspension and distress were natural products of these circumstances. By 1844, all but six of the original sixteen had gone into liquidation.[1]

The reform movement in Louisiana was a direct product of the distress and culminated in a new system in 1842, which deserves to rank with the New York system of 1838. The germ of this reform was a report by Edmond J. Forstall in February, 1837, a document which, taken in connection with his work in modeling the new system, entitles him to rank as one of the keenest financiers of the period.[2] This report, although unduly optimistic over the great valley commerce, nevertheless pointed out that the situation was defective and 'full of hazards.' It explained the necessity of considering both circulation and deposits as threats in a panic. In order to maintain public confidence, it was imperative that banks pay their liabilities on demand. In order to do this, two things were necessary: in the first place, a specie reserve of one third the cash responsibility, called the 'bank movement,' and, secondly, a loan policy based on 'short paper, payable on a fixed day, and moving in a rapid circle.' 'Long paper,' continued the report, 'although perfectly sound, can be of no use to a bank to meet notes or debts payable on demand.' This principle, Forstall thought, was not new, for it was proposed by Albert Gallatin in 1831 and had been the settled policy of the Bank of England. With rare foresight he called attention to the recent action of the Bank of England in attempting to fortify its bullion reserves. For

[1] 29th Cong., 1st Sess., *House Ex. Doc.* No. 226, pp. 833; 839; 842. Those still operating were the Louisiana State, the Bank of Louisiana, Canal Bank, Mechanics and Traders, and the Union.

[2] It appears from the rather scanty information at hand that Forstall was a prominent sugar planter of Louisiana, President of the Citizens Bank, and a member of the Legislature. His report shows a wide reading. The *Bankers' Magazine* in 1877 (XXXII, p. 352), says: 'We have been at pains to inquire of old bank officers in New Orleans as to the authorship of the law of 1842. . . . We are informed that the gentleman most influential in framing the act of 1842 was Edward J. Forristall of New Orleans, for many years the agent of Baring Bros. & Co. of London. His sons are understood to be still the agents of that very eminent house. The father died in 1873 at the age of 80.'

this purpose shortly after June, 1836, it 'proscribed the paper of seven of the most eminent bankers in London, with a view, by contracting suddenly their business, to force the exportation of gold and silver from the United States, to replenish their empty vaults.' [1] The Citizens Bank, unquestionably at the instance of Forstall, had been aware of this action of the Bank of England, and in September and October of 1836, had made arrangements to import large quantities of specie from Havana and Mexico to strengthen the reserves of all the New Orleans banks.[2]

In the session of the Legislature which convened in December, 1837, a bill passed providing for an elaborate reorganization. Although it was vetoed, it deserves attention in tracing the evolution of the reform ideas. It provided for a board of currency composed of three members, each of whom must have been a resident of the State for five years. The board was empowered to make examinations and to require detailed monthly and annual statements of condition. All banks accepting this act as an amendment to their charters were authorized to issue temporary post-notes above twenty dollars payable March 1, 1840, and varying in quantity from twenty per cent of the capital to thirty per cent for the land and utility banks. By March 1, 1839, all must have a ten per cent specie reserve and a year later must have thirty-three and one third per cent. Loans on pledge of stock were limited to thirty per cent, and forty per cent of all loans must be made outside the cities of New Orleans and Lafayette.[3] This bill, however, was vetoed by Governor Ed-

[1] 25th Cong., 2d Sess., *House Ex. Doc.* No. 79, pp. 609–20. *Report of the Joint Committee of Finance of the Senate and House of Representatives, on the Banking Situation of the Moneyed Institutions of New Orleans,* February, 1837. This is a majority report drawn up and presented by E. J. Forstall, chairman of the Finance Committee of the House. Mr. A. Hoa, chairman of the Senate Finance Committee, signed the report.

[2] *Ibid.,* pp. 651–53.

[3] 25th Cong., 3d Sess., *House Ex. Doc.* No. 227, pp. 489–526. The bill in its various stages is given, but the name of the man responsible for it does not appear from the record. It was presented to the Senate by Mr. A. Hoa, who had signed the Forstall report February, 1837. Forstall was a member of the General Bank Committee which presented the revised bill to both houses and was chairman of the sub-committee which prepared an exhaustive analysis of the banking situation on December

ward Douglas White, the father of the late Chief Justice of the United States Supreme Court. Some of its provisions he conceded were good, but he declared, 'the revolution is intended to be a radical one. The Axe is laid at the very root of the tree.' Post-notes he regarded as illegal, the high residence qualifications for directors were too restrictive, violation of vested charter rights was involved, and the distribution of loans over the State showed a distinct 'agrarian tendency.' [1] Some features of this act were doubtless severe, but its major elements showed that the ferment of reform was at work. In 1840, a bill similar in provisions was presented with additional restrictions against engaging in such speculative enterprises as cotton or sugar production.[2] It was not, however, until February 5, 1842, that a bill finally passed marking one of the first steps in thorough reform for the Nation. It is pertinent, therefore, to give a summary of the basic elements of this law, the product of five years of discussion and justly deserving to rank along with the Safety-Fund Law of 1829 and Free-Bank Act of 1838 in New York.

This law provided for a board of currency composed of three members, each being required to be a resident of the State for four years, and neither of whom could be director of a bank, partner of any bank officer, nor a money broker. Each board member was placed under a $5000 bond, to be forfeited by action of the Attorney-General on complaint of any citizen that the duties imposed by law had not been fulfilled. Any suit brought was given summary preference over all others. The board was empowered to examine at will, but not less than four times each year; to require weekly statements of condition and publish them each month, making an annual report to the Legislature. The banks themselves were subject to strict regulations. They must separate their loans into two classes, those made from capital and those from deposits. Capital loans could be made on mortgages,

---

23, 1837. In this he analyzed the types of loans and pressed anew the argument for short paper and reserves. The members of the committee were: A. Hoa, P. E. Bossier, John S. David, E. J. Forstall, Richard Winn, J. Lawson, Thomas H. Lewis, and Felix Garcia.

[1] 25th Cong., 3d Sess., *House Ex. Doc.* No. 227, pp. 527–32.

[2] 29th Cong., 1st Sess., *House Ex. Doc.* No. 226, pp. 645–53; 674–83.

personal security, and other investments 'not realizable in ninety days.' Deposit loans were restricted to ninety-day non-renewable paper, to 'secure a rapid movement in daily receipts.' Capital loans were called 'dead weight'; deposit loans, 'the movement of the bank.' No bank could increase its dead weight so long as its deposits were not protected by thirty-three and a third per cent reserve and sixty-six and two thirds per cent ninety-day non-renewable paper. The board was rigidly to enforce these provisions; any director voting for a loan in violation was personally liable. To prevent the recurrence of the early abuse of speculative enterprise, banks were prohibited from dealing in cotton, sugar, other produce, or stock. A few of the older railroad banks could continue without State obligation to complete their work, but the Gas Light Bank was to sell its interests to the city or a private company without banking powers. All were to resume by September 30, 1842. In the few months between the act and resumption they were empowered to issue a limited number of post-notes under State registry and payable September 30, 1842. These must be secured by fifty per cent specie, and the balance in State bonds, or mortgages taken in ratio of six to five. Daily exchange of notes and weekly specie settlements were required. Each bank must have at least fifty stockholders and none could withdraw a country branch without permission from the Legislature. Any director absent from the State longer than thirty days or from five consecutive meetings had the position automatically vacated.[1] Some five banks eventually accepted these amendments, and became solvent, paying State bonds and relieving the State from the danger of repudiation. By 1850, the Bank of Louisiana had paid all but twenty thousand dollars of bonds issued to it in 1824, and the Union Bank paid shortly afterward.[2]

The Constitution of 1852 empowered the Legislature to create a free-bank system, with notes secured by stocks and a specie reserve. The Louisiana Free-Bank Act was passed on April 30, 1853. This contained certain defects, among

[1] *An Act to Revive the Charters of the Several Banks Located at New Orleans....* February 5, 1842.

[2] *Louisiana Acts* (1850), pp. 7–8.

which was the lack of an individual liability clause, which was remedied in 1855. As finally perfected, it required circulation to be protected by bonds, and deposits by a thirty-three and one third per cent specie reserve, one of the earliest attempts on record of special protection for depositors. Two thirds of all loans were restricted to ninety-day paper, with no investment in real estate.[1] This act was probably the strongest free-bank act in the country, since the standard laws being adopted in the North and West had no special requirement for specie reserves, nor limitation of loans to short-time paper.

NEW ORLEANS IN THE PANIC OF 1857

The strength of the system was never more clearly demonstrated than in the manner in which it withstood the panic of 1857. As the events of the next ten months were to show, it was no mere idle boast when, in January, 1857, the Governor said: 'In such esteem are our monied corporations held that the attention of other States has been attracted to the details of our banking system.'[2] Attempts of a few free banks to inflate the currency on the eve of the panic were suppressed, and all banks in that critical period were held to the laws of 1842 and 1853.[3] The panic coming in other centers in August 'had less effect on the currency in New Orleans than in the other principal commercial marts of the United States.' Of the nine Louisiana banks operating at the time of the panic, five of the largest maintained specie payments on both deposits and circulation throughout the period. The Citizens' Bank temporarily suspended deposit payment on October 14, but assistance was rushed by the other banks so that it was able to resume on November 3. Three of the small free banks suspended both deposits and circulation payments, but due to the assistance of the other New Orleans banks they resumed again early in November.[4] The

[1] Louisiana *Acts*, 1853, pp. 301–11; *Acts*, 1855, *Bankers' Magazine*, VII, p. 996; XII, pp. 735–39.

[2] Louisiana *Documents* (1857), Message of Gov. R. C. Wycliffe.

[3] *Ibid.*, pp. 8–16. *Report of Joint Committee on Banks and Banking*, March 4, 1857.

[4] Louisiana *Documents* (1858), *Report of the Board of Currency*, January, 1858, p. 307.

effective manner in which the system weathered the panic is strikingly shown by an examination of the statistics.[1] It is obvious that depositor fears began to weaken the reserves in the early stages of the panic, but that the ninety-day paper, 'revolving in a rapid circle,' as Forstall had predicted in 1837, began to strengthen the banks' resources and that the accumulating specie was used to pay demand liability. Consequently, by November, bill-holder and depositor nerves were steadied and 'the community became ashamed of the panic before the panic was over,' a psychology not unlike that which William T. Sherman had noted in California two years earlier, or his brother, John Sherman, noted in New York twenty years later.[2]

[1] The following table is compiled from the *Report of the Joint Committee on Banks and Banking*; and the *Report of the Board of Currency* in the Louisiana *Documents* (1858), pp. 26–37; 46–49; and is expressed in the nearest millions of dollars:

Date	Circulation	Deposits	Specie	Ninety-Day Paper
July 25, 1857	9.8	10.2	6.9	16.7
Aug. 29, 1857	8.3	9.6	6.5	18.8
Sept. 26, 1857	7.9	9.8	6.4	20.3
Oct. 10, 1857	7.5	8.5	5.4	20.3
Oct. 12, 1857	7.4	8.2	5.2	20.2
Oct. 13, 1857	7.2	7.9	5.0	19.9
Oct. 14, 1857	7.1	7.8	4.7	19.9
Oct. 15, 1857	6.6	7.3	4.2	19.8
Oct. 16, 1857	6.2	6.8	3.5	19.6
Oct. 17, 1857	6.1	6.5	3.4	19.2
Oct. 31, 1857	5.2	6.6	3.9	18.0
Nov. 28, 1857	4.1	10.0	8.0	15.5
Dec. 26, 1857	4.3	11.5	10.2	15.0

The figures for November 28 and December 26 include two small free banks recently organized but their resources were so small that they did not affect the tremendous recovery shown on those days. In another report 'specie' is listed as 'actual coin' and is shown somewhat smaller than in this table which includes certain small items regarded by the Board of Currency as equivalent to specie. An interesting fact is that in contrast to the period twenty years earlier, the specie held is largely gold.

[2] William T. Sherman, *Memoirs* (2 vols., New York, 1875), I, p. 114. Sherman, working in the bank of Lucas and Turner during a deposit run of 1855, was confronted by a Frenchman demanding his money. When tendered his deposits in gold, however, his face fell, and he is reported by Sherman to have said, 'If you got the money, I no want him, but if you no got him, I want him like the devil.' It will be recalled that on January 1, 1879, when John Sherman collected specie to resume on Civil War

The success of Louisiana banks in warding off the panic of 1857 brought a query from New Orleans, which the editor of the *Bankers' Magazine* thought was exultant: 'Why...has a system of this kind, so thoroughly tested and approved, not been generally imitated?' [1] But the exultation was justified and the query pertinent. Attention was generally directed to the New Orleans system after the panic, and in Massachusetts one feature of it was partially adopted. Under the influence of Samuel Hooper and Amasa Walker, a law was passed in 1858 requiring a fifteen per cent reserve. [2] This was the same Samuel Hooper who in 1860 published a pamphlet comparing the Boston and New Orleans systems and showing that the latter required much higher reserve in addition to a short-paper loan policy, [3] and the same Hooper who pushed the National Bank Act through the House of Representatives. In New York in 1858, Governor King, The Chamber of Commerce, and the Superintendent of Banks recommended reserve provisions of the Louisiana type. [4] Moreover, the Massachusetts' Superintendent of Banks seconded Hooper in commending the New Orleans system. [5] Hugh McCulloch declared that southern Indiana branches had large dealings with New Orleans bankers and 'that cash balances, and the proceeds of commercial paper as it matured were remitted for according to directions — not a

greenbacks, very few people called for specie when it was known that he really had it.

[1] *Bankers' Magazine*, XII, p. 663.

[2] *Ibid.*, p. 734; 782.

[3] Samuel Hooper, *An Examination of the Theory and Effect of Laws Regulating the Amount of Specie in Banks* (Boston, 1860). The *Bankers' Magazine* declares that Hooper had written another pamphlet on 'Money' expressing the same views earlier, and that the reserve provisions of the National Bank Act were copied almost *verbatim* from the Massachusetts law of 1858. (*Bankers' Magazine*, XXXII, p. 351.)

[4] *Bankers' Magazine*, XII, pp. 886–88. Governor King asked for a twenty-five per cent reserve, saying, 'Under a law similar to this, the chief banks in the country were enabled to resist the pressure of universal suspension.'

[5] Massachusetts *Public Documents* (1861), No. 10, p. 127. President Buchanan in his message, December 8, 1857, also alluded to the strength of the Louisiana system. (Richardson, *Messages and Papers*, V (1897), p. 438.)

dollar was withheld. No more able and honorably conducted banks existed in the Union than those of New Orleans before the war, nor was mercantile honor anywhere of higher tone than in that city.' [1]

[1] Hugh McCulloch, *Men and Measures* (New York, 1886), pp. 138–39.

CHAPTER V

BANKS OR NO BANKS

'I DO not dislike your bank any more than all banks. But ever since I read the history of the South Sea Bubble, I have been afraid of banks.' So Andrew Jackson expressed himself to Nicholas Biddle in 1829.[1] To James K. Polk, in 1833, he wrote: 'Every one that knows me, does know, that I have been always opposed to the U. States Bank, nay all Banks,' adding that the original draft of his inaugural message in 1829 contained an expression of this idea which was omitted in deference to advice.[2] It is not necessary, therefore, to suppose that his ideas on the subject were other than those long held, and merely strengthened and confirmed by events.

There was in Jackson's mind both an anti-bank and a no-bank idea. The anti-bank idea, part of a growing anti-corporation attitude widely held, was based largely on a certain fear that large corporations were in some way inimical to a free American individualism. Governor Mason of Michigan in 1835 vetoed a steamboat charter with the statement that 'acts of incorporation are aristocratic in their tendencies.... Individual enterprise is embarrassed and discouraged by them and the efforts of unassisted industry are prostrated by the successful competition of consolidated wealth.'[3] Governor Reid of Florida declared that in 'every corporation there exist elements unfriendly to republicanism.'[4] A New York

[1] John Spencer Bassett, *Life of Andrew Jackson* (2 vols., New York, 1911), II, p. 599. Jackson appears to have acquired his hostility to paper-money banks by noticing the distress in his State of Tennessee, caused by the panic of 1819. Benton came to the same conclusion in Missouri.

[2] *Ibid.*, p. 430. Eugene Irving McCormac, *James K. Polk* (New York, 1922), pp. 26–27. Jackson's *Farewell Address*, of course, expresses the same idea and in a letter to Francis Blair, June 5, 1837, he wrote: 'You know I hate the paper system, and believe all banks to be corruptly administered.' (Bassett, II, p. 725.)

[3] G. N. Fuller, *Messages of the Governors of Michigan*, I, p. 40.

[4] 26th Cong., 2d Sess., *House Ex. Doc.* No. 111, p. 243, January 13, 1840.

committee reported that it was 'a palpable fraud for bankers to pretend that they are democrats, or that any man is a democrat who contends for bank paper.'[1] The panic of 1837 served to strengthen and spread these ideas during the depression of the early forties. Debtor distress was rationalized into a settled hostility to banks and bankers.

The no-bank, hard-money, or bullionist idea, was based on an economic theory rather than an emotion, a theory existing long before the panic of 1837, continuing after the panic of 1857, and held by many sober men both in America and England. It was held by Jefferson as against Hamilton, and by Jackson and Benton as against Biddle and Webster. The idea was thus expressed by an English writer to Amasa Walker: 'You and the hard-money school maintain that nothing but the precious metals can afford absolute security for the transfer of value, whilst I hold that a national bank-note...convertible in specie on demand, is as good a security in public belief as specie itself.'[2] Briefly, then, the bullionist contention was that paper money, as a Galena miner would have said, was not real money but 'cheek'; and was subject to such violent fluctuations as to be impossible to regulate. The credit-money idea held, on the contrary, that credit might rationally be used and that a system could be adopted whereby paper money, convertible into specie, would be equivalent to specie. Thomas Hart Benton, who as a lifelong advocate of hard money, earned the sobriquet of 'Old Bullion,' was the megaphone of the idea. Unsound, however, as his bullionist idea may be as a theory of money, it certainly cannot be called a theory of unsound money in the sense of an inflated currency. Moreover, hard money would undoubtedly have produced more stable values than the paper-money system as it existed in 1837. It was the business of the next twenty years to produce a system of paper money convertible into specie, and it cannot be said that the credit advocates were any more constructive in evolving methods than the bullionist advocates. Indeed, a thesis might well be made that the most constructive bank-

[1] Assembly *Documents* (1837), IV, No. 302, p. 25.

[2] *Bankers' Magazine*, XIV, pp. 497–98. Homer Stanfield to Amasa Walker, Burley, England, September 23, 1859.

ing legislation came in those areas where the no-bank attitudes were strongest, lashed to action under the anti-bank
spur. It should be recalled that constructive ideas were held
by Benton. He pointed out in the debate of the thirties the
lack of individual liability of the United States Bank. Missouri had one of the soundest State banks of the country, and
adopted in 1857 a strong reserve law; and Benton called attention to the general lack of reserve requirements in
America in contrast to the Bank of England.[1]

Furthermore, this no-bank theory was not limited to
America. William Cobbett had, since his Newgate Prison
days in 1810, tilted against the paper-money system in his
Register, in pamphlet, and before Parliament.[2] Laughed
down by Parliament,[3] he came to America in the early
thirties, viewed with a sympathetic eye Jackson's struggle
with the 'money power,' and wrote a biography of him with
the estimate that he had 'never seen, never heard of, and
never read of, any man equal to the President....' [4] Lest it
be supposed, however, that these ideas only germinated on
the fringes, it should be noted that many sober men were
drawn to the bullionist theory — such men, for example, as
Amasa Walker, George D. Lyman, William Gouge, James
Guthrie, S. P. Chase, Edward G. Ryan, and Samuel
Hooper.[5]

It is obvious, then, that there were two ideas — anti-corporation and anti-paper money — not easily distinguished
in the forties. There appears, in fact, to have been a fusion,
or perhaps it was that the anti-corporation elements adopted
the bullionist argument, much as in the seventies and the
nineties with a grand inconsistency they accepted the arguments of inflation. Although the fusion of loco-foco and
bullionist in the forties was a national tendency, it became

[1] *Bankers' Magazine*, XII, pp. 559–65, November 15, 1857.

[2] Lewis Melville, *The Life and Letters of William Cobbett in England
and America* (2 vols., London, 1913), II, pp. 58, 139, 195, 205, 251.

[3] Carlton J. H. Hayes, *Political and Social History of Modern Europe*
(2 vols., New York, 1926), II, p. 110.

[4] William Cobbett, *Life of Andrew Jackson* (New York, 1834), p. v.

[5] The bullionist movement after the panic of 1857 is discussed later in
this chapter.

real only in the Mississippi Valley. In 1846 a Democratic Convention of New York defeated a no-bank proposal by a vote of 78 to 11, while in Wisconsin in the same year, a Democratic Convention adopted a no-bank proposal by a vote of 80 to 24. As a majority movement it was confined to the Mississippi Valley States of Illinois, Wisconsin, Iowa, Missouri, Arkansas, Louisiana, and Texas; and to the Pacific Coast.

THE WISCONSIN IDEA

Banking in Wisconsin Territory at the time of the panic of 1837 was partly an inheritance of the wildcat creations of Michigan and partly the product of its own legislation. Currency was issued by individuals like James D. Doty, by a company chartered to construct a dam across the Fox River, and by other agencies at Green Bay, Milwaukee, and in the lead district.[1] A movement for a State Bank of Wisconsin was started, but its charter was disapproved by Congress.[2] These organizations failed in the panic and by 1841 were in process of liquidation.[3]

From this point until 1853, no banks were created by Wisconsin; and, except an institution which was not legally regarded as a bank, none were in operation. This exception was the Wisconsin Marine and Fire Insurance Company of Milwaukee, which became the focus of the early anti-bank feeling. George Smith, a Scotch emigrant of the thirties, had formerly been engaged in business in Chicago; but after the panic moved to Milwaukee and with some other Scotchmen,

[1] *Report of the Secretary of Treasury on Banks of Wisconsin Territory*, in 25th Cong., 3d Sess., *House Ex. Doc.* No. 232, pp. 1–18; 25th Cong., 2d Sess., *House Ex. Doc.* No. 193, pp. 3–22, contains the text of four charters. Secondary accounts include: M. B. Hammond, 'Financial History of Wisconsin Territory,' in Wisconsin Historical Society *Proceedings* (1894); W. W. Wight, 'Early Legislation Concerning Wisconsin Banks,' in Wisconsin Historical Society *Proceedings* (1895); Clarence Bernard Hadden, 'History of Early Banking in Wisconsin' in Wisconsin Academy of Science, Letters and Arts, *Transactions* (1894); and L. C. Root, 'Early Banks of Issue in Wisconsin,' in *Sound Currency*, V (1898).

[2] 25th Cong., 2d Sess., *Senate Doc.* No. 262.

[3] 26th Cong., 2d Sess., *House Ex. Doc.* No. 111, p. 1, 417; 30th Cong., 1st Sess., *House Ex. Doc.* No. 77, p. 593.

especially Alexander Mitchell, sought a charter for an insurance company. He is reported to have said to Daniel Wells, a member of the Legislature from Milwaukee: 'I know the name of bank is as hateful in your region as a king was in Rome.... The name is a bugbear they detest, but the thing is a boon they need and will welcome. I will sugar the pill.' [1] The charter of February 28, 1839, authorized it to make insurance contracts, accept deposits, and make loans, but expressly said that 'nothing herein contained shall be construed to grant banking privileges.' To its depositors certificates of deposit were issued, which were negotiable, and when passed in the ordinary course of trade soon became the standard medium of Wisconsin and northern Illinois. It is said that only one insurance contract was written, and, by issuing certificates of deposit, an insurance company had in reality been converted into a bank of issue. This 'sugaring of the pill,' however, drew upon George Smith's Bank the fire of the anti-bank men of the forties. As times became harder, their suspicions were confirmed that bankers were shrewd and clever men, and perhaps remembering many another banking subtlety, came to the conclusion that in the language of Francis Bacon banks 'will hardly be brooked in regard of certain suspicions.' Nobody claimed that Smith failed to redeem his certificates on demand; for he had agencies at Chicago, Galena, St. Louis, Detroit, Cincinnati, and Buffalo, and his prompt redemption gained a wide reputation for 'George Smith's money.' The fight against George Smith's Bank culminated in 1846 by the repeal of his charter. He successfully defied the Legislature, however, and despite runs, laws, and investigations continued his business until the general law of 1853. When he entered the general bank system, his circulation was nearly one and one half millions. [2]

Meanwhile, the bank issue had become an important question for the Constitutional Convention of 1846. Before the

[1] James D. Butler, 'Alexander Mitchell, the Financier,' in *Wisconsin Historical Collections*, XI (1888), pp. 435–50.

[2] J. W. Farwell, 'George Smith's Bank,' *Journal of Political Economy*, XIII (1905), pp. 590–93; 'George Smith's Money,' *Sound Currency*, V (1898), pp. 113–20; E. W. Scott, 'Early Banks and Bankers of Chicago,' *Chicago Banker*, I (1899), pp. 14–15.

assembling of the convention the press comments reflected a sharp anti-bank sentiment. The Racine *Advocate* on May 5, 1846, declared that the number of 'bankites' was growing less and it supposed that even the Whigs would oppose any banks. 'Let us hope,' it wrote, 'that the feeling in favor of banks has passed away entirely. But at the same time let us guard against its renewal at some future time.' The Whigs of Dane County, in fact, on July 20, adopted a resolution favoring the prohibition of banks. When the Madison *Wisconsin Democrat* twitted the Whigs for thus adopting Democratic principles, the *Express*, a Whig paper, attempted a lame explanation under the caption: 'What loco-focos can't understand.' The Milwaukee *Sentinel and Gazette* called attention to the New York Convention under Democratic control which had not prohibited banks. It was not a question of banks or no banks, but of well-regulated banks of their own against bad bank paper from the outside.[1]

The first convention was in session from October 5 to December 16, 1846. It consisted of one hundred and twenty-four members, of whom one hundred and three were Democrats and eighteen were Whigs. Of these, forty-nine were farmers, and twenty-six were lawyers. About two thirds of the members originally came from New York and New England. The majority report of the Committee on Banks, presented by Edward G. Ryan, of Racine, on October 9, proposed a sweeping prohibition of banks. Under the proposed article, no bank of issue could operate in the State, nor any other corporation with banking powers, a violation of which was to incur a fine of ten thousand dollars and five years in the penitentiary. Any person receiving notes issued was subject to a fine of five hundred dollars and three months' imprisonment. No corporation was to receive deposits, make discounts, or buy and sell exchange, violation of which incurred a fine of five thousand dollars and two years' imprisonment. A final article empowered and directed the Legislature to enact any further enforcement penalties necessary. Moses S. Gibson, a Whig member of the committee, asserted that the report was prepared by Ryan with-

[1] Milo M. Quaife, *Movement for Statehood*, Wisconsin *Historical Collections*, XXVI, pp. 157–59; 206–10; 261; 380–98.

out a committee meeting and submitted to the members individually. Gibson, while professing strong anti-bank senti-
ments, presented a minority proposal on October 12, which
permitted banks by a two-thirds vote of the Legislature, and
subject to unlimited stockholder liability. During the course
of a long debate on these proposals, it became clear that some
form of prohibition was to be adopted and the question was
mainly the details and the methods. Ryan, who drafted the
extreme anti-bank report, and Moses Strong, who was described as looking 'back to the day when Andrew Jackson
shook his stout hickory shillalah at the Monster,' were leading debaters. As the bank article emerged from the convention in final form, it was the Ryan report amended. The
specific penalties were omitted, but it was strengthened by
sections designed to exclude the branches and paper money
of foreign banks. The article was adopted in the convention
by a vote of 80 to 24.[1] If it were true, as a California dele-

[1] Milo M. Quaife, *Convention of 1846*, Wisconsin *Historical Collections*,
XXVII, pp. 70–71; 92; 139; 201; 744–45. The text of the bank article
was as follows:

'1. There shall be no bank of issue within this State.

'2. The legislature shall not have power to authorize or incorporate,
by any general or special law, any bank or other institution having any
banking power or privilege, or to confer upon any corporation, institution, person or persons, any banking power or privilege.

'3. It shall not be lawful for any corporation, institution, person or
persons within the State, under any pretense or authority, to make or
issue any paper money, note, bill, certificate, or other evidences of debt
whatever, intended to circulate as money.

'4. It shall not be lawful for any corporation within this State under
any pretense or authority to exercise the business of receiving deposits
of money, making discounts, or buying or selling bills of exchange, or to
do any other banking business whatever.

'5. No branch or agency of any bank or banking institution of the
United States or of any State or territory within or without the United
States, shall be established or maintained within this State.

'6. It shall not be lawful to circulate within this State after the year
one thousand eight hundred and forty seven, any paper money, note,
bill, certificate, or other evidence of debt whatever, intended to circulate
as money issued without this State, of a denomination less than $10 or
after the year one thousand eight hundred and forty nine of a denomination less than $20.

'7. The legislature shall at its first session after the adoption of this
constitution and from time to time thereafter as may be necessary enact

gate three years later declared, that banks could 'creep in through an auger hole,' here was an article designed to stop all loopholes.

In addition to serving on several committees and taking part in the debates, Ryan acted as the correspondent for the Racine *Advocate*. The day after the opening of the convention, he was fearful of a soft Tadpole influence from the eastern counties — 'an east wind upon the capitol, redolent of bank or quasi-bank odor.' He supposed that the bank advocates would likely suggest some system of general banking, and on October 8 he wrote: 'Aha! Mr. Mitchell, how would that suit you, eh? Free trade in all things, forsooth, even in swindling the people with shin plasters.' 'A stringent article,' he described his proposal, and when the specific penalties were forced out, amendments were adopted on his motion excluding foreign branches and small bills. A final effort was made by the bank advocates to overthrow the bank article by a reconsideration on November 20, which was refused by a tie vote, and, as Ryan described it, 'You could hear many an anti-bank man draw a long breath of relief' as the vote was announced which finally 'battened down the hatches on banks and banking.' To the Milwaukee *Sentinel and Gazette*, however, this bank article seemed equivalent to a Connecticut blue law.[1]

This constitution was defended by a series of brilliant articles in the Racine *Advocate* after the manner of *The Federalist*, and probably from the pen of Ryan. The article, which appeared 'elaborately careful and in some instances apparently redundant,' was made so because 'experience has taught the framers that the devices and the evasions of the money power are innumerable.' The door, however, was left open for deposit, exchange, and discount conducted by individuals or partnerships. 'But it is said that bank issues may be secured. The answer is that nothing but specie, dollar for dollar, can really secure bank issues.' Neither mortgages nor public security are adequate as shown in New York, where

adequate penalties for the punishment of all violations and evasions of the provisions of this article.'

[1] Milo M. Quaife, *Struggle Over Ratification*, Wisconsin *Historical Collections*, XXVIII, pp. 15; 18–23; 43; 117.

they have depreciated and in the case of a war would still further depreciate.[1] The popular referendum on April 6, 1847, resulted in the defeat of the Constitution by a vote of 20,233 to 14,119, Racine County rejecting the Constitution by a vote of 2474 to 1363.[2] In this rejection the bank issue shared as a cause with other issues such as the judiciary and Negro suffrage.

The second convention was in session at Madison from December 15, 1847, to February 1, 1848, and had a majority favoring banks under restrictions. On December 23, the majority of the bank committee reported an article allowing banks by special acts and unlimited stockholder liability, approved by popular referendums. The minority reported for a general law and limited liability approved by a popular referendum. The final article, which was a compromise between these two views, passed by a vote of 51 to 31.[3]

Although this constitution was ratified in 1848, it was not until 1853 that any bank act emerged from this complicated process. Over the opposition of Governor Nelson Dewey, a general law was enacted and ratified by a referendum before the close of 1852.[4] It was not, however, until early in 1853

[1] Milo M. Quaife, *Struggle Over Ratification*, Wisconsin *Historical Collections*, XXVIII, pp. 495–500.

[2] *Ibid.*, pp. 697–98.

[3] *Journal of the Convention to Form a Constitution for the State of Wisconsin* (Madison, 1848), pp. 60; 341; 617. The article read as follows:

'The Legislature may submit to the voters at any general election, the question of "BANK," or "NO BANK," and if at any such election a number of votes equal to a majority of all the votes cast at such election on that subject shall be in favor of Banks, then the Legislature shall have power to grant charters, or to pass a general banking law.... Providing that no such grant or law shall have any force or effect until the same shall have been submitted to a vote of the electors of the State, and been approved by a majority of the votes cast on that subject at such election.'

[4] *Bankers' Magazine*, IX, pp. 8–33. There is a curious document called a 'mock message,' January 26, 1851, by a so-called people's Governor, William A. Booth. It notes that certain benevolent persons are asking for a banking system. They were only asking the people, says the 'message,' 'to pay them one dollar in real value for one dollar's worth of solemn promises.' His contempt for this led the people's Governor to recommend that power be granted the Legislature to increase the quantity of land 'for the benefit of the farmers.'

that the first bank began business under this act, the State Bank of Madison.[1]

This was the system, then, that Wisconsin had when the National Bank Act was passed. No State bank system, such as was in operation in Iowa, was attempted. It cannot be said, however, that the system passed through the panic of 1857 or entered the Civil War decade with an undepreciating currency. This was due largely to the use of State stocks as a basis of security, which depreciated with the secession of the South.[2]

TWENTY YEARS OF BANK WAR IN IOWA

From 1838, when Iowa was separated from Wisconsin, until 1858, no banks were created either by the Territory or the State. Judging by the experiences of Michigan and Wisconsin, however, this fact must be credited to the distress growing out of the panic of 1837 rather than to any natural restraint of a frontier community. Although no banks were created, one was in operation. This was the Miners' Bank of Dubuque, with a charter granted by Wisconsin Territory in 1836, and intended to serve the lead district along with the Bank of Mineral Point and the Galena branch of the State Bank of Illinois. The Miners' Bank of Dubuque, however, led a hunted existence from the time it began operations in October, 1837, until its charter was repealed in 1845. Although it boasted of maintaining specie payments longer than any bank of the West, it could not avoid the anti-bank storm gathering on the debtor frontier nor escape the fate of many another bank as rumors grew into investigations and charter repeal. It was never a large institution, and, with this exception, paper-money banks did not exist in Iowa un-

[1] 33d Cong., 2d Sess., *House Ex. Doc.* No. 82, pp. 232–42.

[2] 36th Cong., 2d Sess., *House Ex. Doc.* No. 77, p. 249; 37th Cong., 3d Sess., *House Ex. Doc.* No. 25, p. 187. On October 1, 1861, out of a total deposit of securities amounting to $3,181,000, the following stocks were included, which was a considerable decrease since the previous year: Tennessee, $170,000; Virginia, $28,400; North Carolina, $194,500; Georgia, $17,500; Louisiana, $56,000; Missouri, $1,029,000. On April 20, 1861, the New York stock market listed Missouri stocks at 39¾; Virginia, 36½; Tennessee, 41. (Frederick Merk, *Economic History of Wisconsin during the Civil War Decade*, Madison, 1916, pp. 187–219.)

til 1858. Yet, if banks did not exist, the question did, and is best studied in relation to the three constitutional conventions of 1844, 1846, and 1857.[1]

The first Iowa Constitutional Convention, in session October 7 to November 1, 1844, consisted of fifty-one Democrats and twenty-one Whigs, forty-one of the total being farmers. The majority report of the Committee of Incorporations reported an article authorizing 'one bank...with branches, not to exceed one for every six counties.' Additional restrictions included a referendum on bank charters, stockholders to be 'liable respectively' for debts, and charters subject to repeal or amendment at the pleasure of the Legislature. The minority report presented by Stephen Hempstead, a Dubuque lawyer, proposed that 'No bank or banking corporation of discount or circulation shall ever be established in this State.' The minority report was rejected by a vote of 51 to 17, but a study of the debate shows a rising anti-bank feeling with Hempstead leading the anti-bank argument. To exclude banks of circulation, Hempstead said, 'would be carrying out the principles of the great Democratic party of the country.' Banks were institutions designed to 'swindle the people' by lending a fictitious credit which artificially inflated prices until a panic when 'ruin and distress were inflicted upon the community.' 'Human wisdom,' he declared, 'was not able to devise any plan to restrain these corporations, they work together and work in secret. . . . If the whole concern — Banks, officers, and all concerned could be sent to the Penitentiary, he would be very glad of it.' Richard Quinton, a farmer of Keokuk County, declared that banks 'were a set of swindling machines, and now was the time for the people of Iowa to give an eternal quietus to the whole concern.' John Ripley, a farmer of Des Moines County, said they 'were a curse to the country, unconstitutional, and oppressive upon the laboring classes...not long since he had a ten dollar bill — he thought he had ten dollars. He took it to a Burlington merchant to

[1] Howard H. Preston, *History of Banking in Iowa* (1922), pp. 27–34; Fred D. Merritt, 'Early Banking in Iowa,' in University of Iowa *Bulletin* (1900); Hoyt Sherman, 'Early Banking in Iowa,' in *Annals of Iowa*, V (1901); Ivan L. Pollock, *Economic Legislation in Iowa* (1918).

get silver, but the merchant informed him that money was not exchanged for silver without a discount. He was obliged to lose perhaps fifty cents on the bill. He had not ten dollars when he thought he had.' John C. Hall, a Henry County lawyer, originally from New York, declared that 'banking was a spoiled child' which 'conferred privileges upon one class that other classes did not enjoy.... Gentlemen talked about well-regulated banks. They might as well talk about white blackbirds.' He is reported to have declared later that 'a Bank of Earth is the best bank and a plough share the best share.'

Not all farmers nor all Democrats, however, held these views, for a large number favored a system under careful restrictions, general incorporation, and popular referendums. One delegate declared that a Democratic Convention was on the point of making 'as good a constitution as any Whig or banker would want,' and was answered that the vote on the bank question was no 'test vote, that was to prove who in this convention were Democrats.' After a coalition of moderate Democrats and Whigs had voted down the no-bank proposal, attention next turned to the majority report, and the votes upon this show that the moderate reform Democrats insisted on great restrictions. A resolution to strike out the unlimited liability clause was lost by a vote of 52 to 17, only one Whig being in favor of retaining it. A motion to strike out the right to repeal or alter any charter at the pleasure of the Legislature lost by a vote of 69 to 20. A motion to amend the report by declaring it a felony to violate a charter carried by a vote of 37 to 33. The bank article as it emerged from the debate required a two-thirds vote of the Legislature to charter, a twenty-year time limit, unlimited stockholder liability, power to repeal at discretion, and a referendum on any charter. Although Mr. Chapman, a Democratic lawyer, sounded a warning that these anti-corporation restrictions would keep out railroads, a final move to strike out the article lost by 46 to 22, and a motion to substitute limited liability lost by 46 to 20.[1] To the Whig objec-

[1] *Fragments of the Debates of the Iowa Conventions of 1844 and 1846* (edited by B. F. Shambaugh, Iowa City, 1900), pp. 67–102; 140–50. No official journal was kept and this volume is compiled from the daily newspapers.

tion that this constitution was too agrarian, the *Iowa Capital Reporter* replied: 'These soulless monsters have tyrannized long enough, and we rejoice that Iowa... has bound the hydra hand and foot.' [1] This constitution, however, was rejected in April, 1845, by 996 votes, and again in August by a smaller vote, being complicated with a boundary question.[2]

A petition for a Bank of Iowa was presented to the Legislature in 1845 but got short shrift. The *Iowa Capital Reporter* referred to it as an 'incipient little monster,' a 'vampire upon the body politic,' devised for a 'pampered bank aristocracy.' The editor hoped for it 'a warm reception, a summary disposal, and a speedy quietus.' The petition did not emerge from the committee.[3]

The second convention of Iowa, in session from May 4 to May 19, 1846, consisted of thirty-two members, twenty-two Democrats and ten Whigs, with only eight farmers. The *Iowa Capital Reporter* declared that it knew of no nominating convention, either Whig or Democratic, that had instructed its delegates to support a banking system. 'If there is even a *respectable minority* of the people who are really desirous that banks should be established, they are extremely backward in making their wishes known.' The action of the convention prohibiting banks was ratified by a popular referendum in 1846 by a close vote. With only a few sparsely settled counties not counted, the vote was 9942 to 9036.[4] While the Iowa Convention of 1846 prohibited banks, it cannot be said that it did so in such a thorough fashion as the Wisconsin Constitution of the same year.[5] Assuming

[1] Shambaugh, *Fragments*, pp. 225–27.

[2] B. F. Shambaugh, *Constitutions of Iowa* (Des Moines, 1902), pp. 271; 283.

[3] Preston, p. 35.   [4] Shambaugh, *Fragments*, pp. 345; 372.

[5] Thorpe, II, p. 1032. The article read as follows: 'No corporate body shall hereafter be created, renewed, or extended, with the privilege of making, issuing, or putting into circulation, any bill, check, ticket, certificate, promissory note, or other paper, or the paper of any bank, to circulate as money. The General Assembly of this State shall prohibit by law, any person or persons, association, company, or corporation, from exercising the privileges of banking, or creating paper to circulate as money.'

that such a prohibition was possible, the defect of the Iowa article was in its failure to attempt a suppression of the use of paper money from other States. In either case it was likely to be an example of prohibition not prohibiting.

Iowa, therefore, had no paper money of its own creation until authorized by the Constitution of 1857. This constitution was formed by a convention in session from January 19 to March 5, 1857, and ratified by a popular majority of 1630 votes. The convention consisted of thirty-six members, twenty-one Republicans and fifteen Democrats, among whom there were fourteen lawyers and twelve farmers.[1] There was no disposition to continue the prohibition of banks, for a no-bank proposal was defeated by a vote of 31 to 4. The issue was in reality between the advocates of a State bank monopoly and a general bank law. The debate showed a willingness to borrow from the experiences of other States.[2] The final article was a combination of these two views, although there was still a trace of the old anti-bank suspicion in that any charter might be repealed by a two-thirds vote.[3]

In accordance with this constitution, laws were passed in 1858 providing for a State bank and a free-bank system. The charter of the State Bank of Iowa, March 20, 1858, provided for a central board of directors to exercise supervision and control note issues which were to be protected by a twelve and one half per cent safety-fund and a twenty-five per cent specie reserve. Moreover, twenty-five per cent of all deposits were to be retained in the vaults. As far as positive restrictions of law are concerned, this was one of the soundest State banks of the Nation.[4] Its subsequent history proved that its management was equally sound and Iowa escaped the difficulties of other banking systems of the upper Mississippi Valley in the Civil War decade.[5] The general law, March 22, 1858, was equally well modeled. In addition to a note issue protected by high-class securities taken at

[1] Shambaugh, *Constitutions of Iowa*, p. 352.

[2] *Official Report of the Debates and Proceedings of the Convention of 1857* (2 vols., Davenport, 1857), I, pp. 344–60; II, p. 792.

[3] Thorpe, II, pp. 1149–50.

[4] *Bankers' Magazine*, XII, pp. 945–61.

[5] Preston, pp. 83–125.

ninety per cent, a specie reserve to redeem on demand was required, and a twenty-five per cent reserve against deposits.[1] It appears, however, that banks preferred to organize as branches of the State Bank rather than under the general law. As late as 1863, the only banks operating in the State were the fourteen branches of the State Bank.[2] On January 3, 1861, this system held over twenty-five per cent reserve against both circulation and deposits in addition to a large safety-fund.[3]

Despite a long bank war, Iowa, in 1863, might well boast of its system. Was this the product of the anti-bank sentiment? Was the no-bank insistence on hard money an influence in securing a paper money made equivalent to hard money by reserves? If such is the case, then neither anti-bank nor no-bank can be regarded as destructive forces.

EGYPT *vs.* UP-STATE

The collapse of Illinois banks in the depression period following the panic of 1837 has already been discussed. Paper-money banks ceased to exist within the State from 1843 to 1851. Private banks, however, continued dealing in loans, exchange, and deposits. Paper money also circulated from banks without the State, particularly from 'George Smith's Bank' of Milwaukee, the Indiana State Bank, and the Missouri State Bank. As prosperity revived in the later forties and immigration thrust into the northern part of the State, the demand for banks under Illinois regulation was renewed. This movement is reflected in the Constitutional Convention of 1847.

The convention, in session at Springfield from June 7 to August 31, 1847, was composed of one hundred and sixty-two members, of whom ninety-one were Democrats. Farmers numbered seventy-five and lawyers fifty-four.[4] The usual

---

[1] *Bankers' Magazine*, XIII, pp. 31–43.

[2] 38th Cong., 1st Sess., *House Ex. Doc.* No. 20, p. 174.

[3] 37th Cong., 3d Sess., *House Ex. Doc.* No. 25, pp. 167–68. The condition was as follows: Circulation, $689,319; deposits, $1,312,046; reserve, $509,500; safety-fund, $153,940.

[4] Arthur Charles Cole, *The Constitutional Debates of 1847*, in Illinois *Historical Collections*, XIV (1919), introduction.

no-bank articles were proposed, but the majority report of the Committee on Banks and Corporations proposed a referendum on the question which, if favorable, would permit the creation of banks under general laws or special acts, provided that the State held no interest.[1] The forces were fairly evenly divided, for a resolution to prohibit lost by a vote of 74 to 65, while a resolution to prohibit for ten years, with a referendum at that time, lost by one vote.[2] The final action was a victory for the pro-bank party, allowing banks by general or special laws when ratified by a referendum.[3]

After 1848, the question had to be agitated for three years before the Legislature consented to pass a law. The Chicago Board of Trade drafted a bill for a general law and the campaign for banks was supported by the commercial interests in other cities. The Democratic State platform in 1848, however, declared strongly against the move, and Governor French, in his message of January, 1849, was likewise hostile. It was not until the session of 1851 that the pro-bank party was successful, and Governor French and down-State Democrats were defeated by what they were disposed to regard as the Chicago money oligarchy. The vote was close, however, and the law passed in the upper house by the deciding vote of an up-State Democrat, Senator Joel Matteson, later Governor. The act was promptly vetoed by Governor French, who wanted nothing less than total stockholder liability. It was passed over his veto and when submitted to the people in November, 1851, was ratified. The distribution of the vote over the State showed that the issue was as

[1] Cole, *Constitutional Debates*, pp. 312–14.

[2] *Convention Journal* (Springfield, 1847), pp. 288; 410.

[3] *Ibid.*, pp. 564–65. The Constitution containing this clause was ratified by a popular referendum on March 6, 1848. The vote for the Constitution was 60,585 against 15,903. The bank clause read as follows:

' No State bank shall hereafter be created, nor shall the State own or be liable for any stock in any corporation or joint-stock association for banking purposes to be hereafter created.

' No act of the general assembly authorizing corporations or associations for banking purposes, shall go into effect, or in any manner be in force, unless the same shall be submitted to the people at the general election next succeeding the passage of the same, and be approved by a majority of all the votes cast at such an election for and against such a law.'

much a sectional one between northern and southern Illinois as it was an issue between Whig and Democrat. The popular majority for the law was fifty-four per cent, with only four counties north of Sangamon voting against, while counties around Cook went for the law by majorities of eighty-five to ninety-five per cent.[1]

The act of 1851 as it finally passed this complicated process established a free-banking system on the New York model, although it was less carefully drawn in the matter of the quality of securities deposited.[2] The system passed the panic of 1857 satisfactorily, with only six failures, in which the bill-holder ultimately lost in only one. The Governor and the bank commissioners declared in 1859 that the system had stood the test of the panic.[3]

What finally destroyed the Illinois system was not so much a defect in principle as the Civil War. In January, 1861, approximately seventy-five per cent of Illinois currency was secured by the bonds of States already seceded or threatening to do so.[4] As these bonds depreciated with the approach of war, the authorities made repeated calls for additional security. In February, 1861, the system was overhauled by limiting future security to Illinois bonds,[5] but this did not save it. By April 7, 1862, eighty-nine banks had failed. The securities of four of these were sufficient to redeem at par, but the redemption rates of the others ranged from ninety-five to fifty per cent. The total circulation shrank from twelve million dollars to one half million.[6] These figures

[1] Arthur Charles Cole, *The Era of the Civil War* (Springfield, 1919), pp. 94–98. The vote of 1851 is plotted and reveals the sectional conflict. The veto message of Governor French is in the Illinois *House Journal* (1851), pp. 474–77.

[2] *Bankers' Magazine*, IX, pp. 449–66; text of the law.

[3] Cole, *The Era of the Civil War*, pp. 99–100.

[4] 36th Cong., 2d Sess., *House Ex. Doc.* No. 77, p. 214, January 11, 1861. At that time Illinois currency amounted to $12,320,694. Southern bonds deposited consisted of: Missouri, $3,026,000; Tennessee, $3,321,-000; Virginia, $1,284,000; Louisiana, $507,500; North Carolina, $888,-000; South Carolina, $100,000; Georgia, $335,000; Kentucky, $66,000.

[5] *Bankers' Magazine*, XV, pp. 793–803.

[6] 37th Cong., 3d Sess., *House Ex. Doc.* No. 25, pp. 161–62. The circulation was $538,711. Southern bonds had been reduced to $10,000.

measure the collapse of the free-bank system and help explain the explosion of anti-bank wrath which swept over the State. A final effort to stabilize the currency by a Union Bank of Illinois based on the State Bank of Indiana was a failure, for the law was rejected in the election of November, 1861.[1] At the same election delegates for a constitutional convention were chosen and the Democrats won a sweeping victory.

The convention, in session at Springfield from January 7 to March 24, 1862, consisted of forty-five Democrats, twenty-one Republicans, and nine Independents. It met under the suspicion of the Republican minority, which was disposed to regard the Democratic majority as plotting treason, organized under down-State leaders, deliberated under the eyes of a regiment of militia, and produced a constitution which the minority promptly dubbed 'the Egyptian swindle.'[2] In addition to gerrymandering the State and forbidding the immigration of Negroes or the right of suffrage to those already domiciled, the convention dealt in drastic manner with banks, the Illinois Central Railroad, and corporations in general. The bank article was fully as drastic as that of the Wisconsin Convention of 1846. It provided that 'no bank, banking corporation, nor any association, or corporation with powers of circulation, or deposit, or any other powers' should be 'revived, enlarged, extended or renewed'; 'no bank bill, check, draft, note, or other written or printed instrument' under ten dollars issued 'within or without' the State might be circulated after 1862, none under twenty dollars after 1864, and none of any denomination after 1866. The Legislature at its first session following was directed to pass an enforcement act with criminal penalties; the auditor was to cease issue of free-bank currency under the law of 1851; and the Legislature was to drive out existing bank-notes by a direct tax. Furthermore, all corporations dealing in discount, deposit, exchange, or loan were prohibited. This article was adopted in convention by a vote of 38 to 23.[3]

[1] *Bankers' Magazine*, XV, pp. 777-92.

[2] Cole, *The Era of the Civil War*, p. 267; O. M. Dickinson, *Illinois Constitutional Convention of 1862*, University of Illinois *Studies*, I.

[3] *Convention Journal* (Springfield, 1862), pp. 937-38. The tax claus

From March until June 17, when the popular vote was taken, the debate proceeded with great excitement. John Wentworth, a Cook County Republican leader, spoke for the Constitution; Owen Lovejoy, and John Reynolds, a former Democrat, spoke against it. The *Chicago Tribune* dealt with it on election day under the caption: 'Down with the Secession Constitution.' The Constitution was defeated by the close vote of 16,051 majority, but the bank article, which was voted on separately, lost by an even smaller vote. The soldier vote taken in the field contributed materially to the rejection.[1]

When the National Banking System was established, Illinois had experienced a quarter-century of bank war. Beginning with the fight on the two banks in 1837, they had been forced into liquidation by 1843. Before banks could again be established, the issue was fought out in the Convention of 1847, the referendum of 1848, and in the Legislature for three years. A law was passed, vetoed, enacted over the veto, and submitted to a referendum in 1851. The collapse of the system in 1861 caused a revival of the war, and saw a proposal for a Union Bank defeated in a referendum, and the whole process of controversy repeated in the convention and referendum of 1862.

OTHER STATES OF THE NORTHWEST

Elsewhere in the Northwest there was a tendency to conform to the prevailing anti-bank reactions, but with varying results. Michigan, sobered by her wildcat experiences, was in an anti-bank mood and her Constitution of 1850 provided drastic restrictions. Banks might be created under general laws or a single bank with branches might be established by a two-thirds vote of the Legislature. But all charters

was adopted by a vote of 43 to 11. It should be noted that individuals or partnerships not issuing paper money could operate under this clause, but they would have no advantage of limited liability.

[1] Cole, *The Era of the Civil War*, pp. 267–72. The fact that the clauses dealing with Negro suffrage and immigration carried by such overwhelming votes as 176,271 and 107,650 would make it appear that the real issue was the economic one. Down-State counties, had they voted with as much strength as they did in November, 1861, would easily have carried the Constitution.

could be repealed or amended, and both 'officers and stockholders' were subject to unlimited liability.[1] Even with these drastic restrictions no opportunity was afforded to banks until the free-bank law of 1857 was ratified by a referendum, November 2, 1858.[2] Although a constitutional amendment in 1860 reduced the liability to the standard single liability,[3] only four small institutions were reported in 1861.[4]

A constitutional convention of Missouri in session from November 17, 1845, to January 14, 1846, was controlled by the no-bank forces. A bank article was written which directed a divorce of the State and the existing State Bank, prohibited any more banks, and subjected all other corporations to unlimited stockholder liability.[5] This constitution was defeated in referendum, however, and possesses no significance except as a mirror for the reactions.

In Minnesota no system of banking was established prior to 1858. Private banks operated, the American Fur Company at St. Paul provided such services as deposit and exchange,[6] and paper money circulated from banks without the State. The prevailing mood, however, was anti-bank. The Governor's message in 1852 declared that 'in the peculiar conditions of society in an early stage of its political existence banking is extremely hazardous.'[7] In 1854, the Governor threatened to veto any charter,[8] and a movement to establish a Bank of Minnesota failed.[9] The Convention of 1857

[1] Thorpe, IV, p. 1964.

[2] *Bankers' Magazine* XIII, pp. 241–53.

[3] Thorpe, IV, p. 1974.

[4] 37th Cong., 1st Sess., *House Ex. Doc.* No. 25, p. 172.

[5] *Journal of the Convention of the State of Missouri* (Jefferson City, 1845), Appendix, pp. 52–53.

[6] A. O. Eliason, 'Beginning of Banking in Minnesota,' in Minnesota *Historical Collections*, XXI, pp. 673–75; Sidney A. Patchin, 'Development of Banking in Minnesota,' in Minnesota *Historical Collections*, II, pp. 111–58. A bank of issue is reported at St. Paul in 1849 and another operated by Borup and Oakes in 1854.

[7] Minnesota *Council Journal* (1852), pp. 22–23.

[8] *House Journal* (1854), p. 29.

[9] *Council Journal* (1854), pp. 69; 121–22. Text of the bill is in *House Journal* (1854), pp. 295–304.

was controlled by fifty-eight Republicans against fifty-five Democrats, but the bank article adopted was a restrictive one. A free-bank system might be established by a two-thirds vote of the Legislature, but stockholders were to be liable for double the amount of their stock.[1] Such a free-bank system was established by a law of July 26, 1858.[2] Banks established under this act, however, were not very successful. The Governor pronounced the system a failure and recommended repeal.[3] The auditor reported that out of sixteen authorized, only seven banks were in operation. He declared that 'the want of confidence so generally diffused with reference to banks and bankers makes it difficult to organize any system of credit represented by paper promises....' He concluded that 'no system can be adopted authorizing the issue of paper currency that will prove of public benefit.' [4] William M. Gouge, who, as a clerk in the Treasury Department, was charged with the duty of collecting information on State banks, viewed this as a confirmation of his hard-money theories.[5]

The attitude toward banks in Kansas is reflected in the bank clauses of the various rival constitutions. The Topeka Constitution of 1855 provided for a free-bank system, the Lecompton Constitution of 1857 for a single bank and branch system, and the Leavenworth Constitution of 1858 for a free-bank system. The Wyandotte Constitution of 1859 adopted the free-bank idea with the important principle that a ten per cent specie reserve be maintained.[6] By an act of June 4, 1861, a free-bank system was adopted,[7] but as late as 1863, only two small institutions were reported.[8]

In Nebraska the suspicion of banks was less than the desire

[1] Thorpe, IV, pp. 2013–14.

[2] *Bankers' Magazine*, XVI, pp. 17–21.

[3] Minnesota *Senate Journal* (1859–60), pp. 15–16.

[4] 36th Cong., 1st Sess., *House Ex. Doc.* No. 49, p. 291.

[5] *Bankers' Magazine*, XIV, p. 7.

[6] Thorpe, II, pp. 1193; 1213; 1237–38; 1256–57; George W. Martin, 'A Chapter from the Archives,' in Kansas *Historical Collections*, XII, pp. 359–75.

[7] Kansas *Laws* (1861), pp. 88–100.

[8] *Bankers' Magazine*, XVII, p. 29.

for them; and from 1855 to 1857, charters for banks and insurance companies with banking privileges were passed, vetoed, and reënacted with such reckless abandon as to recall the wildcat days of Michigan.[1] The panic of 1857, however, played havoc with these banks, and in 1860, Governor J. Sterling Morton declared: 'the Platte Valley Bank of Nebraska City is the only unbursted bank in the Territory of Nebraska. The banking system of this Territory is loose and dangerous and has been a curse to our people.'[2]

LOWER MISSISSIPPI VALLEY

The State of Arkansas, entering the Union on the eve of the panic of 1837, was caught in the tide of inflation and the pressure is mirrored in the very words of its Constitution. It provided for a State bank to act as a repository of State funds, which were to be loaned 'throughout the State, and in every county in proportion to the population.' Another institution was authorized 'to aid and promote the great agricultural interests of the country.'[3] The new State proceeded to charter two banks as the first acts of its first Legislature — the Real Estate Bank and the Bank of the State.[4]

The Real Estate Bank was a typical land bank of the variety discussed in Florida and Mississippi, the State providing the capital by a bond issue. This was lent to farmers on long-time mortgages and the profits were expected to pay the

[1] *Council Journal* (1855), pp. 132–40; *ibid.* (1856), pp. 48–54; *House Journal* (1857), p. 18; Nebraska State Historical Society, *Proceedings and Collections*, 2d Series, IV, pp. 27–31; A. G. Warner, 'Sketches from Territorial History — Wild-Cat Banks,' in Nebraska State Historical Society *Transactions and Reports*, II, pp. 22–39.

[2] 36th Cong., 2d Sess., *House Ex. Doc.* No. 77, p. 508.

Mr. Henry W. Yates, an Omaha banker of the period, estimated that the per capita circulation in 1857 was one hundred dollars in a farming population of about twenty thousand. He recalls that few notes were in circulation and none of the banks in operation by 1861. (Henry W. Yates, 'Early Nebraska Currency and Per Capita Circulation,' in Nebraska State Historical Society *Transactions and Reports*, I, pp. 67–76.)

[3] Thorpe, I, p. 285.

[4] W. B. Worthen, *Early Banking in Arkansas* (Little Rock, 1906), pp. 4–18; 43–51. The author was receiver for the Real Estate Bank when its affairs were finally settled in 1880.

interest and retire the bonds by 1861. The bank began operations at its main office in Little Rock on December 12, 1838,
and by the following April it had four branches: at Helena,
Columbus, Washington, and Van Buren. Before the close of
1839, however, it suspended specie payments and at the
same time inflated its circulation and loans. But on July 1,
1841, it failed to pay interest on the State bonds issued and
the obligation fell upon the State.[1] The bank was placed in
liquidation under a board of trustees by deed of assignment
of the stockholders on April 2, 1842. In 1855, however, this
board was succeeded by a receiver appointed by the State.
From 1855 to 1880, it was in gradual process of liquidation.[2]

The Bank of the State was capitalized by a bond issue and
various State funds, such as Surplus Revenue, the five per
cent federal donation of the proceeds of public land sales,
and Seminary funds. It was no more successful, however,
than the land bank and was placed in liquidation in 1843.[3]
The Bank of the State failed to pay interest on the bonds
issued to it on July 1, 1841.

Arkansas finally met all its obligations arising from these
banking ventures except the $500,000 of so-called Holford
bonds. These were issued to the Real Estate Bank to establish a western branch and one hundred stockholders gave
mortgages on 65,125 acres. The bank was unable to sell them
in 1840, but was able to use them as collateral for a loan. On
September 7, 1840, it pledged them to the North American
Trust and Banking Company of New York for a loan of
$121,336.59. These bonds were subsequently disposed of by

[1] 33d Cong., 2d Sess., *House Ex. Doc.* No. 82, pp. 174–82. Message of
Governor E. N. Conway, November 7, 1854. Bonds to the amount of
$1,530,000 bearing interest at six per cent and due October 26, 1861, had
been issued. As security for these, the 180 stockholders had given the
State mortgages on 141,980 acres. The so-called Holford bonds, amounting to $500,000, are not included in this total.

[2] Worthen, p. 32; Charles Hillman Brough, 'The Industrial History
of Arkansas,' in Arkansas Historical Society *Publications*, I, pp. 209–11.

[3] Worthen, pp. 43–51; 29th Cong., 1st Sess., *House Ex. Doc.* No. 226,
pp. 902–06, Report of Auditor E. N. Conway, November 4, 1844. A total
of $1,169,000 State bonds had been issued to this bank; part of these were
five per cent bonds due January 1, 1887, and payable at New York;
$1,000,000 were due January 1, 1869, one half payable at London and
one half in New York, bearing interest at six per cent.

the New York bank to James Holford, of London. When the Real Estate Bank failed, the question was whether the State was obligated to pay the holders of these bonds in full. The argument was made that the bank had illegally disposed of them below par.[1] By a funding act of April 6, 1869, the entire State debt was recognized and the Holford bonds included.[2] In the end, however, these bonds were repudiated and the Constitution of 1885 carried an article prohibiting payment.[3] Inexperience and enthusiasm, which pictured the profits from these banks as providing the revenue for the State Government, education, and plantation expansion, devolved a heavy burden on the State. The attempt to coin the wild lands of Arkansas failed, bankers became suspected, and credit money regarded as a swindle. The State joined the anti-bank movement of the West and by an amendment to its Constitution in 1846 provided that 'no bank or banking institution shall hereafter be incorporated in this State.' [4]

Although Texas was not politically a part of the United States, its banking development was very similar to that of the American frontier, and it was caught in the maelstrom of inflation in the very year of independence. Before the panic, numerous internal improvement organizations with banking privileges were chartered, ranging from one to construct a hotel and bath-house to the gigantic Texas Railroad Navigation and Banking Company. The latter was to have a capital of $10,000,000 and was authorized to issue paper money in addition to constructing railroads and a canal from the Sabine to the Rio Grande.[5]

[1] 34th Cong., 3d Sess; *House Ex. Doc.* No. 87, pp. 158–65; Report of Accountants, William M. Gouge and William Miller, October 20, 1856.

[2] T. S. Staples, *Reconstruction in Arkansas,* in Columbia University *Studies,* CIX (1923), pp. 347–49.

[3] Thorpe, I, p. 372.

[4] *Ibid.,* I, p. 287. The Secretary of the Treasury had invested some funds of the Smithsonian Institution and certain Indian funds in Arkansas bank bonds. The Federal Government made these investments good by withholding the five per cent public land donation fund.

[5] William M. Gouge, *Fiscal History of Texas* (Philadelphia, 1852), pp. 59–66. This work was written by a man for a number of years connected with the United States Treasury Department. He was an

Not only did the panic arrest further improvement banks, but it produced suspicion of those already chartered, and many immigrants fleeing from the distress of the lower South contributed to swell the anti-bank ideas. An attempt to repeal the charter of the giant Railroad Navigation and Banking Company called forth a committee report which duplicated the American frontier attitude. Banks, said the committee, 'were calculated to control and direct the operation of the Government, if ... not totally to subvert and overthrow its Republican character. If, by the power which wealth alone can wield, the Rothschilds have been able to make the sovereigns of Europe subservient to their purposes, what may we not calculate as the result of such an operating machine as this colossal charter.... In this charter are contained provisions which inevitably produce a powerful monied aristocracy....' [1] An attempt was made to solve the financial difficulty by an issue of Treasury notes, but these depreciated on the New Orleans Exchange to fifty cents, and President Houston vetoed a subsequent issue.[2] President Lamar, in his message of December 24, 1838, recommended a National Bank with a circulation secured by public lands, but in January, 1839, a bill to carry out this proposal was defeated.[3] An attempt was next made to float a loan in the United States and in Europe, but General Hamilton, who had been sent to Europe for this purpose, discovered that the repudiation threats of the States was a serious obstacle.[4] 'No period,' he said, 'could possibly be more unpropitious for all financial negotiations founded upon securities from our side of the Atlantic.' It was his opinion that a loan was impossible

avowed no-bank advocate and expressed his views in a number of books, notably *A Short History of Paper Money and Banking in the United States* (Philadelphia, 1833), which was republished by William Cobbett in England under the title *The Curse of Paper Money*. Despite his prejudices and positive judgments he had first-hand information of conditions in Texas and Arkansas.

[1] Republic of Texas *House Journal* (1836–38), pp. 180–82. Report of the Judiciary Committee, November 24, 1837.

[2] *Ibid.*, pp. 119–31, May 12, 1838.

[3] Gouge, pp. 87–96.

[4] George P. Garrison, *Texan Diplomatic Correspondence*, in American Historical Association *Annual Report* (1908), II, pp. 905–06.

without a National Bank, 'a real effective organ of public credit, not a mere paper manufactory.'[1]

Efforts to establish a National Bank failed, and a movement to repudiate Treasury notes was manifested; but Houston, now serving his second term as President, denounced repudiation and renewed negotiations for a European loan. This proved futile, however, and by 1844 the anti-bank men were in the majority. President Jones urged, on December 9, 1844, 'the entire abolishment of paper money issue by government, corporations, or individuals and the consequent introduction of an exclusive hard money currency.'[2] It was in this mood that Texas formed her Constitution of 1845 and was admitted to the Union.

This convention, dominated by the Jacksonian tradition, showed clearly that the Republic was a part of the American frontier. Mr. Rush, President of the convention, in the course of the debate said: 'The gentleman from San Patricio says that many people have been benefited by banks. Thousands upon thousands, Sir, have been ruined by them. I consider it a bright page in the history of General Jackson that he had the honor of giving the blow which will eventually destroy them on the continent. And I wish by no vote of mine here or elsewhere to authorize the institution of a bank, which may profit a few individuals, but will carry want, misery, ruin, and degradation in its train.'[3] The Constitution adopted showed the dominance of this attitude, for it carried the following clause: 'No corporate body shall hereafter be created, renewed, or extended with banking or discounting privileges.'[4]

Despite this Constitution, one bank of issue continued to exist — the Commercial and Agricultural Bank of Galveston.

[1] Am. Hist. Assn., *Annual Report* (1903), pp. 1287; 1341. John Horsely Palmer, ex-President of the Bank of England, prepared a plan for a National Bank of Texas which Hamilton forwarded to the Texan Minister at Washington for publication and to President Lamar. (*Ibid.*, 1907, II, p. 493; April, 1841.)

[2] Gouge, pp. 113–29.

[3] F. L. Paxson, 'The Constitution of Texas,' *Southwest Historical Quarterly*, XVIII, pp. 386–98.

[4] B. P. Poore, *Charters and Constitutions* (2 vols., Washington, 1877), II, p. 1778.

This institution was chartered April 30, 1835, by Mexico. Since the panic of 1837, it had been a defunct organization, but the Constitution of 1845 gave it a monopoly in the State. The Attorney-General sought to compel it to cease business, but the Texas Supreme Court upheld the validity of its charter as a vested right antedating the Constitution.[1] Therefore, since its charter ran until 1855, Texas could not evade one small monster.[2]

A constitutional convention of Louisiana in 1845 was controlled by the no-bank forces. The pro-bank party proposed to allow bank charters after six months' publicity, provided that all charters granted be subject to amendment or repeal and that stockholders be liable *in solido* for the debts of the corporation. This proposition, drastic as it was, met with immediate opposition, and the no-bank clause was carried by a vote of 38 to 19. Others wished to go further and make it a criminal offense to circulate paper money issued without the State. One delegate declared: 'if we are to put down banking let us put it down effectually, and ... return to the good old system of hard money.' This attempt to proscribe foreign paper lost by a vote of 31 to 25. An effort was next made to drive out the small bills of the five existing banks, operating under the law of 1842. To effect this, it was proposed that existing banks issue no bills under ten dollars after 1847, none under twenty dollars after 1848, and none under fifty dollars after 1849. This was defeated by a vote of 37 to 15.[3] The final clause, adopted May 14, and ratified by referendum November 5, was a no-bank triumph and intended to place the State on a hard-money basis after the expiration of the existing charters.[4] This no-bank clause could not last, however, in such a commercial community as Louisiana and it is not surprising that the Convention of

[1] 32d Cong., 2d Sess., *House Ex. Doc.* No. 66, p. 281; *Bankers' Magazine*, VII, pp. 329; 594–96.

[2] 34th Cong., 1st Sess., *House Ex. Doc.* No. 102, p. 216.

[3] *Proceedings and Debates of the Convention of Louisiana* (New Orleans, 1845), pp. 848–49; 860–62.

[4] Thorpe, III, p. 1405. The clause read as follows: 'No corporate body shall be hereafter created, renewed, or extended with banking or discounting privileges.'

1852 undid the work of 1845. The new Constitution, ratified November 1, 1852, gave authority to create banks by special or general laws, but notes issued must be secured by public securities and ample security in specie.[1] The free-bank system of 1853 is discussed elsewhere.

THE PACIFIC COAST

The rush to California brought to that area a group of men already hostile to paper money, and the abundance of gold from the mines strengthened their belief that real money could be felt in the pocket and be heard to jingle. This animus was shown in the debates of the convention which assembled at Monterey in September, 1849. The committee that drafted the bank article presented two proposals; one a majority report for deposit banks under general laws, the other a minority report proposing unequivocal prohibition of all banks. The debate turned upon the proposed deposit banks, their advocates disclaiming any ulterior purpose of introducing banks of issue in disguise. The anti-bank men, however, feared such would be the case, recalling, no doubt, George Smith's Bank at Milwaukee and Aaron Burr's Manhattan Company at New York. J. C. Botts, a Virginia lawyer, expressed the fear that 'this insinuating serpent, a circulating bank, will find its way through.' 'I fear,' he continued, 'that without being aware of it, this vigilant enemy is near them, they may find bank men in this country, and they are the sharpest and the shrewdest of men. I tell you, Sir, these banks can creep in through an auger hole.'[2] The final action of the convention allowed deposit banking under general laws, but it carefully provided that their certificates of deposits could not circulate as paper money. The Legislature was directed to make the issue of paper money a criminal offense.[3] A law was passed in 1855 providing a fine of

[1] Poore, I, pp. 735–36.

[2] *Debates in the Convention of California* (Washington, 1850), pp. 108–36; R. D. Hunt, 'Genesis of California's First Constitution,' in Johns Hopkins University *Studies*, XIII (1895), pp. 407–12; Cardinal Goodwin, *The Establishment of State Government in California* (New York, 1914), pp. 178–92.

[3] Thorpe, I, p. 396.

two thousand dollars and three months in jail for the first
offense and from one to five years' imprisonment for the
second.[1] Banking in California, therefore, was limited to
deposit, discount, and exchange, and no banks of issue were
introduced until after the Civil War.[2]

Hostility to paper money was likewise shown in early
Nevada. As early as 1861, the laws of the Territory prohibited the issue of paper money.[3] The Constitutional Convention at Carson City in 1864 also showed a sharp suspicion
of paper money. An article was reported providing that 'no
bank-notes or paper of any kind shall ever be permitted to
circulate as money in this State, except the Federal currency
under the laws of Congress.' Debate developed into the following exchange:

> *Mr. Hovey.* I move to strike out that section.
> *Mr. Nourse.* What is the object of that?
> *Mr. Banks.* So that we can have banks here if we want them.
> *Mr. Nourse.* And paper money?
> *Several Members.* Yes, paper money.
> *Mr. Nourse.* Well, I go against all such stuff.[4]

In Oregon the Constitution of 1857 prohibited banks of
issue,[5] so that on the Pacific Coast the first banks of issue
were those established under the National Bank Act, but the
preference for hard money continued for many years.

BULLIONIST THEORY AFTER THE PANIC OF 1857

As already noted, the idea that credit money was a swindle
was current long before the no-bank movement of the forties.
Thomas Jefferson, who declared that banks of issue were
'more dangerous than standing armies,' and John Adams,
who held that every bank-note issued, without an actual

[1] *Statutes of California* (1855), p. 128.

[2] Benjamin C. Wright, *Banking in California 1849–1900* (San Francisco, 1910). *Bankers' Magazine*, XV, pp. 49–63, gives the names and
locations of private bankers in June, 1860. William T. Sherman in his
Memoirs also gives interesting views of early banking in California.

[3] *Laws of Nevada Territory* (1861), p. 88.

[4] *Debates and Proceedings of the Constitutional Convention of Nevada*
(Carson City, 1864), pp. 163–65.

[5] Thorpe, V, p. 3013.

specie basis, 'represents nothing and is therefore a cheat upon somebody,' were in accord with Andrew Jackson and Thomas Hart Benton.[1]

The idea persisted, moreover, after the movement in the West to abolish paper money by law had subsided. The panic of 1857 stimulated a revival of bullionist discussion accompanied by many constructive suggestions. George Tucker, an economist who had argued so cogently for a system of regulated credit money in 1839,[2] was somewhat doubtful in 1858. He conceded that the repeated bank suspensions went far to justify the hard-money advocates; yet he thought that 'it would be both easier and better to reform than abolish.' His suggestions, at several points the same as those of 1839, were very constructive. He proposed a limitation of notes and deposits to a fixed proportion of the actual specie in vaults and a restriction of loans and discounts to short paper. Jackson's idea of suppressing small bills under twenty dollars, Tucker thought, was a good one; and he was now disposed to accept the free-bank principle of bond security.[3] Thomas Hart Benton, long an advocate of hard money, called attention to the reserve requirements of the Bank of England in contrast to the general American practice.[4] Amasa Walker, of Massachusetts, was the most noted economist supporting the hard-money theory.[5] The fact that he and Samuel Hooper pushed through a law in the Massachusetts Legislature of 1858 requiring a fifteen per cent reserve is proof of the constructive force of the bullion-

[1] H. E. Miller, 'Banking Theories in the United States Before 1860,' Harvard Economic *Studies*, XXX (1928), pp. 19–20.

[2] George Tucker, *Theory of Money and Banks Investigated* (Boston, 1839), pp. 205–07. He wrote: 'The most effectual restriction would be one which should compel them to regulate their loans and issues by the amount of specie in their vaults.' The English practice of a thirty-three and a third per cent reserve was his suggestion. He did not think, however, that the New York free-bank principle was a sound one, differing in this respect from Condy Raguet and Eleazar Lord.

[3] George Tucker, 'Banks or No Banks,' in *Hunt's Merchants' Magazine*, XXXVIII (February, 1858), pp. 145–57.

[4] *Bankers' Magazine*, XII, pp. 559–65, November 15, 1857.

[5] Amasa Walker, *Nature and Uses of Money and Mixed Currency* (Boston, 1857). Many articles by Walker will be found in *Hunt's Merchants' Magazine* and *Bankers' Magazine* after 1857.

ist theory.[1] George D. Lyman, Manager of the New York
Clearing House, declared that 'the sooner we return to the
exclusive use of the only legal money of the country, the
sooner shall we be relieved from the evils of revulsions,
panics, and general periodic bankruptcy.'[2] James Guthrie,
Secretary of Treasury, was of the opinion that the Fathers
were hard-money men and that paper money was unconstitutional.[3] John A. Dix, soon to be a Secretary of the
Treasury, declared: 'The only legitimate currency for any
country is coin, and until within the last two centuries,
there was no other. Paper money, which professes to be a
representative of specie, and redeemable in it, is a contriv-
ance of modern speculators.... So long as it represents an
equal amount of specie, securely placed, for which it can be
exchanged, it is unobjectionable if issued in considerable
sums.... A bank-note for one hundred dollars, for instance,
is more conveniently carried about the person, or sent from
one place to another, than the gold or silver coin which it
represents.' He supposed, however, that the complete bullionist theory could not now be adopted, and proposed in
lieu thereof to suppress small bills under twenty dollars or
fifty dollars and establish a bullion bank which would issue
certificates of deposit on an equal amount of coin.[4] Such a
bullion bank, in fact, was organized in New York in 1859 with
such prominent men among its directors as John A. Dix, B.
H. Field, and George Opdyke. It had a capital of one million
dollars, accepted deposits, all of which were kept in the
vaults. Profits were expected to accrue from capital loans
and a commission charge on deposits.[5] Charles H. Carroll, of
Boston, argued that, before the time of the Bank of England,
banks had been mere deposit institutions, such institutions
as those of Venice issuing no credit money. He saw no good
reason for the change.[6] William M. Gouge, long connected
with the Treasury Department and for over a quarter-

[1] *Bankers' Magazine*, XII, pp. 734; 782.

[2] *Ibid.*, October 28, 1858.

[3] *Ibid.*, November 3, 1858, pp. 596-98.

[4] *Ibid.*, XIII, pp. 513-23.   [5] *Ibid.*, pp. 440-52; 757-60.

[6] *Ibid.*, pp. 673-77; 833-42; *Hunt's Merchants' Magazine*, XXXVII,
pp. 307-12; 429-34; XXXVIII, pp. 33-42.

century a consistent opponent of paper money, was still a
hard-money man.[1] Salmon P. Chase, as Governor of Ohio in
1858, had his doubts concerning paper money,[2] and curiously enough in the very report in which he urged upon
Congress the National Bank Act used the following words:
'If a credit circulation in any form be desirable, it is most
desirable in this.' [3]

[1] *Bankers' Magazine*, XIV, pp. 3–9.

[2] *Ohio Messages and Reports* (1858), pp. 357–59, January 4, 1858. He
conceded 'the convenience of a mixed currency of coin and convertible
notes, and the improbability that a currency entirely of coin will soon
be adopted.' He favored a National law suppressing notes below twenty
dollars, and called attention to the need of deposit protection.

[3] *Congressional Globe*, Appendix (1861–62), p. 26.

CHAPTER VI
PASSING THE NATIONAL BANK ACT

THIS chapter will consider the problem of the immediate origins of the National Bank Act during the Civil War, a difficult and controversial question of personal contributions. The purpose will be to present the conflicting claims rather than pronounce a judgment. A review of the evidence will emphasize the definite contacts between the National System and the State systems, and, it is hoped, afford a basis for a tentative opinion.

THE CHASE RECOMMENDATION

The first official act looking toward the establishment of a National System was the report of Chase, December 9, 1861. In this he considered two finance proposals: (1) the issue of Treasury notes, redeemable in coin, and (2) the establishment of a National Bank System with a note issue secured by 'the pledge of United States stock, and an adequate provision of specie.' The former he was not prepared to advise, but the latter plan he definitely recommended as being based on the practical experience of New York. The question arises: Did the plan originate with Chase, or was it suggested to him? The idea may well have originated independently with the Secretary, for it will be recalled that Ohio had a strong system in which the bond-security feature was used as well as the specie reserve. Moreover, Chase, as Governor of Ohio at the time of the panic of 1857, obviously had studied the system of his State and his message of 1858 showed constructive thought. The expression, 'an adequate provision of specie,' in the report of 1861, was not a product of the New York System, and may well have come from a study of the Ohio laws and a hard-money background. However this may be, it is certain that several suggestions of a National currency secured by bonds had been made prior to the report of Chase. No less than five such suggestions had been made by men familiar with the New York idea.

Two of these were made by direct letters to Chase, and one in person.

FILLMORE-BONNEFOUX SUGGESTION

As early as 1848, Millard Fillmore, then Comptroller of the Currency in New York, had suggested the idea. After expressing the hope that the New York free-bank principle might be generally adopted by other States, he continued: 'If, then, in addition to this, Congress would authorize such notes as were secured by stocks of the United States, to be received for public dues to the National treasury, this would give such notes a universal credit, co-extensive with the United States, and leave nothing further to be desired in the shape of a national paper currency. This would avoid all objection to a national bank, by obviating all necessity for one for the purpose of furnishing a national currency. The National Government might be made amply secure. The law might provide that all bills secured by United States stock should be registered and countersigned in the Treasury Department, as the notes circulated by the banks of this State are registered and countersigned in this office.' [1] This suggestion, however, fell on stony ground and appears to have had no immediate effect other than to get itself denounced as a Whig bank scheme.

In 1861, Laurent Bonnefoux, an experienced New York merchant and financier, revived the Fillmore suggestion. Under date of October 11, 1861, he wrote: 'the next Congress cannot hesitate to take up in earnest the question of creating a NATIONAL CURRENCY'; and in December, 1861, he presented his views at length in the *Bankers' Magazine*. By his own statement, he had been an advocate and student of the New York principle since its establishment. This system, however, as originally created, he regarded as defective, in

[1] Buffalo Historical Society *Publications*, X, pp. 282–83, December 30, 1848. Perhaps Condy Raguet had this in mind in 1839 when he said that the New York principle was 'better calculated, if made general throughout the Union, to give stability to the currency, than any other that would be likely to meet a general acceptance.' (*Currency and Banking*, Philadelphia, 1839, p. 212.) See also Isaac Bronson, *Letters addressed to Levi Woodbury* (1837), advocating a National Bank with notes secured by bonds.

that it permitted the use of mortgages and the poor stocks of other States. He came to the conclusion that the proper method was to limit securities to New York stocks, and in November, 1838, organized upon this principle the New York State Stock Security Bank. He fought a movement in 1847 which proposed to substitute the Safety-Fund System for the bond-security principle. He claims to have inspired the Fillmore report of 1848 and to have defended that suggestion by articles in the *New York Evening Post*.[1]

POTTER PLAN

In August, 1861, Orlando B. Potter, of New York, addressed a letter to Chase with the outline of a plan for a 'national bank currency, based upon and secured by, the national stocks.' Under this plan, existing banks were to continue under State regulation, but were to be encouraged to use National bonds for their notes. A United States Superintendent of Banking was to be created to receive deposits of bonds, and issue thereon a National currency; and it was hoped that eventually this currency would displace the State bank issues. 'The plan,' said Potter, 'will be fully understood by an examination of the statutes of this State regulating the security of the circulations by our banks, by deposits with the State.'[2]

LORD PROPOSAL

Another member of the New York group who suggested the bond-security principle was Eleazar Lord, who claims to have suggested the idea of the original New York law in 1829.[3] In November, 1861, in a letter to Chase, Lord sug-

[1] L. Bonnefoux, 'Financial Policy of the Government,' in *Bankers' Magazine*, XVI, pp. 417–50.

[2] Orlando B. Potter, *Plan for Appreciating the National Bank-Notes to the Value of Coin, Without Diminishing the Volume of the Currency. Also, His Plan of the National Bank Currency Based upon, and Secured by the National Stocks, Submitted to Secretary Chase Aug. 14, 1861* (New York, 1875). See also his *National Currency, Its Origins* (New York, 1883); and his speech in Congress, in *Congressional Record*, January 15, 1885.

[3] The essay which Lord claims suggested this principle was, *Credit, Currency, and Banking* (New York, 1829, and 1834). One must beware,

gested a National currency based on a deposit of United States bonds with the Treasury Department. His suggestion, however, was not for a currency redeemable in specie on demand, but for one convertible into United States bonds which were redeemable in specie some twenty years hence. The bill, drawn by him, specifically provided that 'no obligation shall be imposed on any Banking Company or Association... to redeem with gold or silver, or otherwise, the notes so secured and circulated by them.' His proposal was, therefore, for a legal-tender issue on the credit of the Government.[1]

STILWELL-JORDAN CLAIM

An active member of the New York group was Silas M. Stilwell, who came to Washington in 1861 and urged his views on Chase in person. Stilwell had been active in New York politics for more than thirty years, and claimed credit for the National Bankruptcy Act, the New York law abolishing imprisonment for debt, and the New York Free-Bank Law of 1838.[2] Moreover, in 1874, he claimed that 'During

however, of assigning the New York idea to any particular person, for the same difficulty exists here as in the case of the National law. Silas M. Stilwell claims to have inspired the law and Dickson Ryan Fox credits it to a certain Willis Hall. Another writer traces the idea back as far as 1815; D. B. Waldo, 'Origin of the National Banking System,' in Michigan Political Science *Publications*, I. One may neglect the antiquarian problem to point out the important fact that both Lord and Stilwell were in contact with both systems.

[1] Eleazar Lord, *A Letter on National Currency* (Pierpont, New York, November 22, 1861); *Six Letters on the Necessity and Practicability of a National Currency, and the Principles and Measures Essential to It* (New York, 1862). This is a pamphlet opposing the bill then before Congress. The objection appears to have been that this bill, perhaps the original Hooper Bill, required specie redemption.

[2] *A Report of Two Interviews with Honorable Silas M. Stilwell* (Chicago, 1874). The claims of Stilwell regarding the law of 1838 are open to question. In the New York *Assembly Journal* (1838), p. 725, for March 26, 1838, appears this record: 'The memorial of three hundred and eighty-five citizens of the County of Niagara, praying for the passage of an act to establish the business of banking on the principle recommended by the Honorable Silas M. Stilwell, was read, and referred to the standing committee on the incorporation and alteration of the charters of banking and insurance companies.' This plan was no doubt the one

the years 1861 and 1862 I prevailed upon Mr. Chase... to ask Congress to adopt for the United States a Free Bank law of the State of New York....' [1] This claim was repeated in 1879. Congressman A. H. Buckner, of Missouri, Chairman of the Committee on Banking and Currency, had been in correspondence with Stilwell and had asked the direct question: 'Who is the author of the National Banking Law?' In reply to this question, Stilwell forwarded a clipping from the *New York Graphic*. This was the report of an interview with Edward Jordan, Solicitor of the Treasury under Chase. Jordan is reported as giving the following statement:

'Late in the year of 1862, in December I am quite sure, Secretary Chase introduced me to Silas M. Stilwell of New York City, asking that I should hear Mr. Stilwell's views in regard to a national system of banking....

'Mr. Stilwell spent two or three days in elaborating his views with me, as he had previously done with Judge Chase, and concluded by submitting a draft of a bill embodying them.... I was directed by Judge Chase to prepare a bill.... I prepared a bill, using Mr. Stilwell's materials.' [2]

---

contained in a pamphlet entitled, *A System of Credit for a Republic and the Plan of a Bank for the State of New York* (Albany, 1838). This plan, however, proposed a giant loan bank with a note issue based on land security, a type of bank like those being established in the Cotton South.

[1] *A Report of Two Interviews with Honorable Silas M. Stilwell* (Chicago, 1874). This purports to be answers by Stilwell to reporters of the *New York Times* and the *Chicago Inter-Ocean* and refers to him as 'the confidential adviser of the Treasury Department during the early years of Secretary Chase's incumbency.' He is represented as saying that the National System was only a partial adoption of his idea. He did not favor limiting circulation to $300,000,000. He held that the currency was unduly contracted; that it should increase as the population grew. In a lecture in New York in November, 1865: *National Finances, A Philosophical Examination of Credit* (New York, 1866), he maintained that the National System was copied from New York, but with the fundamental difference that the former restricted the *quantity*, while the latter secured the *quality* of circulation.

[2] *Private History of the Origin and Purpose of the National Bank Law and System of Organized Credits for the United States* (New York, 1879). This is a pamphlet containing Stilwell's letter to A. H. Buckner, April 20, 1879. It so impressed a group of New York men that a committee was appointed to solicit funds for a Stilwell Memorial. The appeal for contributions was approved by such men as Edward Jordan, Thurlow

It seems clear that both Jordan and Stilwell were mistaken in the date that Stilwell came to Washington. Instead of his being there in December, 1862, he was in contact with Chase prior to December, 1861.[1] It may be assumed, therefore, that Stilwell was in Washington prior to December, 1861, that he conferred with Chase, and prepared a pamphlet which was printed by the Government Printing Office. How far his influence was effective, however, is problematical. Here again the important point is the definite contact between the New York law and the National System. Moreover, there is additional evidence of this contact in the columns of *The National Intelligencer*.[2]

SPAULDING-HOOPER BILL

The recommendation of Chase was under the consideration of a sub-committee of the Ways and Means Committee of the House. This consisted of E. G. Spaulding, Erastus Corning, and Samuel Hooper, all practical financiers. Spaulding was President of the Farmers and Mechanics Bank of Buffalo and remained its President long after it was reorganized under the National System. Corning was a merchant, banker, and railroad man of Albany. Hooper was

Weed, the Chancellor of the University of New York City, the Post-master, the Editor of the *Scientific American*, and the Superintendent of Police.

[1] Stilwell in his letter to Buckner gives a detailed but somewhat incoherent account of his relations with Chase. He represents himself as urging upon the Secretary the issue of legal tenders which Chase objected to as unconstitutional. Since the legal tenders were actually issued in February, 1862, Stilwell could not have been urging this measure in December, 1862. Moreover, Stilwell speaks of a pamphlet which he prepared to popularize the idea of a National Banking System. There is such a pamphlet entitled *Notes Explanatory of Mr. Chase's Plan of National Finance* (Washington, Government Printing Office, 1861). This pamphlet has no name attached, but it is clearly the one referred to and is credited to Stilwell by the catalogue of the Library of Congress.

[2] *The National Intelligencer*, January 20, 1862. An anonymous contributor, whom the editor called 'an intelligent banker of New York,' wrote in favor of the plan on December 23, 1861. The editor was obviously receiving many suggestions which lack of space prevented him from printing. He did, however, find room for extracts from Lord's pamphlet, and the readers were reminded of the Fillmore suggestion, which was printed in full.

a merchant, financial writer, and director of a large Boston bank. According to Spaulding, the Chase report reached the committee about the middle of December, 1861. Spaulding, thereupon, addressed a letter to Chase asking for a draft of the bill. On December 18, the Acting Secretary replied that Chase was in New York. 'On the return of the Secretary from New York,' continued Spaulding, 'it was ascertained that no National currency bank bill had been prepared. The Secretary then requested Mr. Spaulding to prepare a bill at as early a day as possible. Mr. Spaulding, as chairman of the sub-committee, immediately set to work at his rooms at the National Hotel, in preparing the first draft of the bill, which was then copied by Mr. George Bassett, Clerk of the Committee of Ways and Means. This was during the Christmas holidays....' In preparing this bill he used the New York laws sent from Albany by Corning on December 26, 1861. When nearly completed, it was submitted to Hooper, who rendered 'valuable assistance in perfecting the bill' by incorporating features drawn from Massachusetts experience.'[1]

HOOPER-SHERMAN CONTRIBUTION

During 1862, Samuel Hooper was the most active man in official life working for the law. He seems to have acted independently of the committee and perhaps against its wishes. He had been aware of the possibility of National action since 1858, for a report to the Massachusetts Legislature of that year, which he signed and perhaps wrote, declared: 'If the States which have hitherto been permitted to continue the system do not heed the demands for some reform...the National Government may assert rights and exercise a power that will bring the Banking Institutions throughout the country under a double and complicate jurisdiction.'[2] In the course of a speech on the Treasury Note Bill, February 3, 1862, he took occasion to urge the adoption of a National

---

[1] E. G. Spaulding, *History of the Legal Tender Paper Money* (Buffalo, 1869), pp. 7–14. He made substantially the same points in a Centennial speech at Philadelphia, *One Hundred Years' Progress in the Business of Banking* (1876). Hooper, it is likely, had more influence than Spaulding suggests.

[2] *Bankers' Magazine*, XII, p. 734.

law. A bill, he said, was under consideration in the Committee on Ways and Means.[1] On July 11, 1862, he introduced a bill in the House.[2] Some five thousand copies of this bill were printed,[3] but it perished in committee. In December, 1862, Chase renewed his recommendation,[4] and the proposal now received the endorsement of Robert J. Walker, ex-Secretary of the Treasury.[5] Samuel Hooper again introduced the bill in the House on January 8, 1863,[6] which with certain amendments became the National Bank Act. It passed in the House, February 20, by a vote of 78 to 64.[7] In the meantime, however, it had been introduced in the Senate by John Sherman, January 26, 1863, and passed, February 12, by a vote of 23 to 21.[8]

CONCLUSION

Who, then, was responsible for the National Banking System? It is clearly impossible to be conclusive. It would appear that it was the work of no one man, but of several.

[1] *Congressional Globe* (1861–62), pp. 615–16.

[2] *Ibid.*, p. 3258.

[3] A pamphlet entitled *The National Currency*, dated July 15, 1862, is unquestionably the bill introduced by Hooper. Another pamphlet entitled *Banking Association and Uniform Currency Bill... Submitted to Congress in December, 1861, and December, 1862*, is largely a duplicate. A comparison of this Hooper Bill with the final National Bank Act establishes the fact that the Hooper Bill was the basis of the National System. The two most important features added were the individual liability clause and the limit of $300,000,000 on circulation.

[4] 37th Cong., 3d Sess., *Senate Doc.* No. 1.

[5] Robert J. Walker, *Review of Our Finances and the Report of Secretary S. P. Chase* (New York, 1862).

[6] *Congressional Globe*, p. 226. This bill was referred to the committee, where Thad Stevens opposed it. It then appears to have been taken to the Senate, where under the leadership of John Sherman it was passed. It was then returned to the House and passed without being referred to the committee.

[7] *Ibid.*, p. 1118.

[8] *Congressional Globe*, pp. 505; 820; 897. A leading opponent in the Senate was Powell of Kentucky. He moved to require a twenty-five per cent specie reserve, which was lost by a vote of 24 to 14. He next moved to make notes receivable for customs, and redeemable in specie twelve months after the war. Sherman opposed all these motions and the latter lost by a vote of 18–18.

The final act was virtually the bill introduced by Samuel Hooper on July 11, 1862, and January 8, 1863. It was also undoubtedly the bill referred to by Hooper in his speech on February 3, 1862. Moreover, in all probability, it was the bill which Spaulding, with the assistance of Hooper, wrote in December, 1861. Whether the Spaulding-Hooper draft was an independent product or was based on the Jordan-Stilwell draft, the evidence does not permit a conclusion. By the statement of Spaulding there had been no draft prepared previous to his; but by statements of Jordan and Stilwell there had been a previous draft. Aside from this question, the man most active in Congress was Samuel Hooper, and it is clear that his hand was upon the bill as early as December, 1861. Moreover, his background affords ample basis for the opinion that he was aware of the necessity of National action and that he was capable of offering valuable assistance in writing such a law.[1] The testimony of Secretary Chase on

[1] Samuel Hooper (1808–75), was born at Marblehead, Massachusetts, of a family which since Colonial days had been prominent in New England business. His father was president of the Marblehead Bank and the owner of vessels engaged in the China trade. Samuel, after experience upon his father's ships, became a partner of the shipping firm of Bryant and Sturgis. Later he became the partner of William Appleton, his predecessor in Congress. He served in the Massachusetts Legislature both in the Senate and the House. As a member of the Senate, he was chairman of the Committee on Banking and was associated with Amasa Walker, the veteran hard-money economist, in enacting the Reserve Law of 1858. Hooper was a Whig and a Republican, but with distinct leanings toward the Democratic doctrine of hard money. His views on the theory of money were expressed in two works: *Currency or Money; its Nature and Uses and the Effects of the Circulation of Bank-Notes on Currency* (Boston, 1855); and, *Specie Currency; the True Interests of the People* (Boston, 1855). E. R. Hoar said of him (*Congressional Record*, February 20, 1875) that he was a Whig who first attracted notice by 'the defense of the doctrine of hard money and the stringent regulation of whatever substitute therefor might be devised, which brought him for a time somewhat in affiliation with the Democrats.' In 1860, he published a pamphlet, *An Examination of the Theory and Effect of Laws Regulating the Amount of Specie in Banks*, in which he compared the Boston banks unfavorably with those of New Orleans. His reputation for finance was strong enough to secure his appointment on the important Committee of Ways and Means in his first term in Congress. The *Bankers' Magazine*, in an article on the *Louisiana Law of 1842* (*Bankers' Magazine*, XXXII, 1874, p. 351), said of Hooper: 'It was not until 1858

this point is important. He wrote in 1874: 'Only Mr. Hooper of Massachusetts, a gentleman whose sound judg-ment and large knowledge of financial subjects, gave great and deserved weight to his opinions...encouraged me by open support. Out of Congress, R. J. Walker, distinguished by his brilliant administration of the Treasury, and by his great ability, gave the plan sanction of his approval.' [1]

that the specie reserve law of Massachusetts... was passed. The author of that law was Samuel Hooper, then a leading merchant of Boston, and a member of the State Senate as Chairman of its Bank Committee. He was ably seconded by Amasa Walker, the veteran political economist. ... Though a director of the largest bank of that city his views were not shared by the great body of Boston bankers. They were generally of the old Whig party and regarded Mr. Hooper as a theorist, dangerously tainted with Democratic nonsense about hard money.... The reserve provision was copied almost verbatim into the national law.'

[1] J. W. Shuckers, *Life and Public Services of S. P. Chase* (New York, 1874), p. 292.

CHAPTER VII
PRINCIPLES OF THE NATIONAL BANKING SYSTEM AND THEIR ORIGINS

THE NATIONAL BANKING SYSTEM was established originally by an act of Congress, approved February 25, 1863. Its principal features may be summarized as follows: (1) creation in the Treasury Department of the office of Comptroller of the Currency, charged with the duty of general administration; (2) incorporation of National banks under general regulations; (3) provisions for the security of a uniform, registered National bank-note circulation by (*a*) deposit of United States bonds with the Comptroller of the Currency, notes to be delivered to the banks to an amount of ninety per cent of the market value of the bonds deposited, such bonds to be held in trust and subject to forfeiture and sale, the proceeds to be applied exclusively to the redemption of notes of insolvent banks; (*b*) a minimum reserve equal to twenty-five per cent of the aggregate liability on circulation and deposits, such reserves to consist of 'lawful money' in vaults, or such fluid assets as clearing house certificates and demand deposits in the principal financial centers; and, (*c*) liability of the individual stockholder in his private capacity to an 'amount, at par value, of shares held, in addition to amount invested in such shares.' National bank-notes were to be legal tender for all obligations of the Government, except interest on the public debt, and for all obligations to the Government, except duties on customs. The most important principles were: (1) general incorporation; (2) a bond-secured note issue; (3) reserves for notes and deposits; and (4) individual stockholder liability.[1]

---

[1] A. M. Davis, 'Origins of the National Banking System,' in National Monetary Commission *Reports*, V (1910), pp. 155–202. Text of the original National Bank Act. The act placed a limit of $300,000,000 on notes which were to be apportioned over the country on the basis of population and 'existing bank capital, resources, and business.' This limitation was removed after the resumption of specie payments, but it was a standing grievance of the West.

The first Comptroller of the Currency was Hugh McCulloch. He had for almost thirty years been engaged in banking in Indiana and was at the time of his appointment President of the Bank of the State of Indiana, one of the largest and soundest banks in the Nation. Since the National law provided at first for the voluntary conversion of the State systems, it was necessary to enact additional legislation, and a series of amendments was passed between 1864 and 1866. Finally the notes of State banks were driven out of circulation by a ten per cent direct tax — an exercise of power upheld by the Supreme Court in the case of *Veazie Bank vs. Fenno.*

This National System was not a restoration of the Second United States Bank which Andrew Jackson had disestablished; nor was it, in any essential feature, indebted to that institution.[1] True, it was an exercise of National control; but the principles of this control had developed in State experience since the panic of 1837. The problem passed from State to Nation just as the problem of regulation of railroads was later to do. As Secretary Chase said in urging the new system upon Congress, it was based on practical State experience, principally of New York.[2] This experience, which has

[1] J. T. Holdsworth and Davis R. Dewey, 'The First and Second Banks of the United States,' in National Monetary Commission *Reports,* IV (1910), pp. 267–81. Texts of charters of First and Second United States Banks. A comparison of the charter of the Second Bank with the National Bank Act shows no essential debt. The limitation on real estate investment appears in both, but it was a standard limitation in the strong State banks also. Part of the capital of the Bank, as was true of the Bank of England, was invested in Government securities, but these were not held as a pledge for circulation.

[2] *Report of the Secretary of Treasury,* December 9, 1861, in *Congressional Globe* (1861–62), Appendix, p. 26. Chase said the system 'has the advantage of recommendation from experience. It is not an untried theory. In the State of New York, and in one or more of the other States, it has been subjected, its most essential parts, to the test of experiment, and has been found practicable and useful.' In some respects it was less restrictive than many State systems. State laws required bank-note redemption in specie, and in general the legal reserves were higher. I am unable to agree with the statement of Professor David S. Muzzey that, 'Though...the Second Bank was overthrown by the election of 1832, the most important features of Hamilton's scheme... were revived in the stress of the Civil War and have remained a part of

been the subject of preceding chapters, will here be summarized.

GENERAL INCORPORATION

Prior to the panic of 1837, the normal method of incorporation for all business had been by special legislative act.[1] It was a method which followed the precedents of the great trading companies of the eighteenth century, the various companies chartered for the settlement of America, the Bank of England, and the First and Second United States Banks — a method based on the theory of established monopoly. As a method of incorporation, however, it was open to serious objections. With the growth of the corporation as a form of business organization in the nineteenth century, a special charter for each was an obsolete method, consuming the time of legislative bodies with administrative detail, creating a medley of corporation law, and inviting charges of corruption and favoritism. The natural solution, arising from necessity of adjustment to economic change, was incorporation under general laws and supervision by special administrative bodies.

Aside from the necessity of administrative reform was the deeper problem of monopoly in an age impregnated with the theory of *laissez-faire* and fast moving in practice everywhere toward the disestablishment of all forms of privilege. Monopoly, no doubt, had demonstrated its value as a method for the social control of credit: as shown in England, in the United States Bank, and in such powerful State systems as those of Massachusetts, New York, South Carolina, and Indiana. It was inevitable, however, that such 'monsters' should arouse opposition in the days of Jacksonian Democracy. From the fuller knowledge of to-day it can be argued, of course, that the era of Jackson made no clearer distinction in finance than in civil service between monopoly as a considered policy and as a special privilege. But of

our policy ever since.' (*The American Adventure*, 2 vols., New York, 1927, I, 160 n.)

[1] A. K. Kuhn, 'Comparative Study of the Law of Corporations,' in Columbia University *Studies*, XLIX (1912), p. 99, assigns the first general incorporation law to Connecticut in 1837.

whatever type, monopolies did not thrive, and many sober men felt the force of the Jacksonian view. Millard Fillmore, Whig President of the United States, defended general incorporation in New York; Albert Gallatin, able Secretary of the Treasury, witnessed without horror the disestablishment of the Second United States Bank; Robert Dale Owen, of Indiana, brilliant son of Robert Owen, justified Jackson on the issue of monopoly; Nathan Appleton, practical financier of Boston, said a National banking monopoly was 'wholly contrary to the spirit of our institutions'; and Daniel Webster, great advocate of the Second Bank in the struggle of the thirties, came to refer to it as 'an obsolete idea.' [1]

The issue of monopoly existed, moreover, long before the duel of Jackson and Biddle. Since the days of the Stuarts, monopoly had grated harshly on the Anglo-Saxon ear, was interdicted by the common law, and condemned by Physiocratic thought. The last vestige of privilege held by the British East India Company was abolished in 1847, and the monopoly of the Bank of England was destroyed by joint-stock banks. Nor did the issue rest in America with the creation of the National System. The new system itself was called a monopoly by the economist Henry C. Carey for placing a limit on bank-note circulation; the term 'money trust' was heard long after that limitation was removed, and recent writers have drawn parallels between Wilson's demand for a 'democracy of credit' and Jackson's fight in the thirties.[2] And the debate is not yet adjourned as the movement toward 'bank mergers' grows. It is not the purpose to judge the merits of this debate, but to suggest that in Jackson's day it was a problem with deep roots and a lively

[1] Nathan Appleton, *Remarks on Currency and Banking*, (Boston, 1841), p. 30. Where no reference is given, statements are based on preceding chapters of this study.

[2] W. E. Dodd, *Woodrow Wilson and His Work* (New York, 1920), p, 140; Charles A. Beard, *Rise of American Civilization* (2 vols., New York, 1927), II, pp. 579; 607. Beard says that in 1913 'the currency and banking system was overhauled in a spirit somewhat Jacksonian,' by 'combining Jacksonian hopes with more financial propriety'; Carter Glass, *Adventure in Constructive Finance* (New York, 1927), p. 111. He says 'the ghost of Andrew Jackson stalked before my face and haunted my couch for nights.'

future — an issue with historical validity about which men might reasonably differ.

The rejection of monopoly in the regulation of banking, however, brought forward the problem of an alternative policy. Complete *laissez-faire* was clearly impossible; although Henry C. Carey, inconsistently enough for a great Protectionist, saw no more reason for restricting 'who shall not issue his note than there is for regulating who shall grow potatoes.' [1] George Tucker, Condy Raguet, and Albert Gallatin had no difficulty in pointing out the fallacy of this position, and the experience of Michigan demonstrated the practical difficulty. Clearly, the way out was not in turning from regulated monopoly to 'wildcat free-banking.' Nor was the solution to be found in the other extreme by the destruction of bank credit and a return to 'constitutional hard money.' This solution, although defended by many men in Europe and America, was obviously impossible in a society each year becoming more industrial. It is easy to show, also, that the attempt to solve it by constitutional enactment was inconsistent with the dominant individualism of the day. Yet a later generation which approached another economic problem by 'trust-busting,' and which has not yet solved the social and economic problem of price stabilization, may well withhold its scorn. If the anti-monopoly and hard-money ideas of Jackson's veto message of July 10, 1832, are beneath contempt, as a close student of the Second Bank has somewhat sharply observed,[2] the future influence of those ideas should not escape the notice of historians. William Cobbett, once a Tory but later no friend of Tories, concluded that the economic and political order of English society was weighted

[1] H. E. Miller, *Banking Theories in United States Before 1860.*

[2] Ralph C. H. Catterall, *Second Bank of the United States* (1903), p. 239. McDonald, in *Jacksonian Democracy* (1906), p. 310, says: 'On financial matters, especially banking and currency, the ideas of Jackson are in the main so crude as to be unworthy of serious consideration save for the momentous consequences which followed their promulgation.' He continues, however: 'Yet one cannot but feel that... Jackson, nevertheless, had hold of the right end of the matter in every one of the great issues of his administrations. His attack on the bank was brutal, but the bank nevertheless was a gigantic monopoly whose abatement was of inestimable benefit to the political and economic life of the country.'

against the masses. An admiring biographer of Andrew Jackson, the veteran British Laborite, adopted the hard-money idea and put it forward in the face of ridicule. With the Bank of England in suspension, Cobbett appears to have been interested in hard money as a social experiment method with the aim of preventing price fluctuations. It is fair to suppose that the hard-money theorists in America were interested in the same thing.

There was, here, a problem to be constructively thought out. The solution was free banking as defined by Robert Dale Owen — 'a restricted or general system.' It was a solution which offered a constructive alternative to the Hamiltonian monopoly, a solution in harmony with the hopes of an obscure pamphleteer of 1834, who wrote: 'We are for abolishing all monopoly, and for substituting in the place of a National Bank a National System of Banking.' [1]

Three men, intimately connected with the establishment of the new system, were impressed by the contrast between it and the old bank. Mr. O. B. Potter, of New York, who wrote Chase in August, 1861, and outlined the main features based on the New York system, said that 'none of the objections justly urged against a United States bank lie against this plan.' [2] Samuel Hooper, who led the fight for the new system in Congress, declared that it 'secured all the benefits of the old United States Bank without many of those objectional features which aroused opposition. It was affirmed that by its favors, the Government enabled that bank to monopolize the business of the country. Here no such system of favoritism exists.' [3] And Chase, in his report of December, 1861, declared that the plan might be adopted 'without risking the perils of a great money monopoly.' General incorporation, adopted into the National Banking System and working its way to Nation-wide adoption after the Civil War, was Jacksonian in origin and import.

[1] H. E. Miller, quoting from a pamphlet by W. R. Collier, *Essay on the Currency in which is Proposed the Enactment by Congress of a General Bank Law* (Boston, 1834).

[2] Davis, 'Origins of the National Banking System,' in National Monetary Commission *Reports*, V (1910), pp. 45–48.

[3] *Congressional Globe* (1861–62), p. 616, February 3, 1862.

BOND-SECURED NOTE ISSUE

The fundamental principle of the National System was a note issue secured by a deposit of bonds with the Comptroller of the Currency. This principle was derived, not from the Second Bank, but from the New York system of 1838, as imitated by other States.[1] As a method of security, it had its virtues as well as its defects. It offered, in the first place, the basis of a reasonable compromise between the prevailing theories of hard money and credit money. Advocates of a credit circulation could argue that, by this principle, paper money circulated as a representative of an equal value of collateral. The banker was thus freed from the bullionist demand that he maintain against notes an equal reserve in coin. He had merely to deposit bonds or other securities which provided a productive investment and, at the same time, protected his notes.

But the defects of the principle were equally clear — some capable of legislative remedy, others inherent in the system. Securities deposited provided an ultimate reserve rather than an immediate asset like coin, and notes tended to fluctuate in proportion to the quality of the collateral and its availability. In New York this defect had been remedied by strengthening the quality and quantity of the collateral security, by excluding bonds of States which repudiated or were delinquent on interest, and by reserving to the Comp-

[1] The experience covered in this study shows the following States as having adopted the free-bank system: Iowa, Michigan, Illinois, Louisiana, Ohio, Indiana, Wisconsin, Massachusetts, Minnesota, Kansas, and New York. The following States in addition to those covered had adopted the system: Vermont (*Bankers' Magazine*, VI, p. 757); Connecticut (*ibid.*, VII, 164); Pennsylvania (*ibid.*, XIV, p. 937); New Jersey (William Nelson, *Public Archives of New Jersey* in American Historical Association *Report*, 1903, I, p. 509); and Tennessee (*Bankers' Magazine*, VI, p. 763). The system was also adopted by Canada (L. C. Root, 'Canadian Bank-Note Currency,' in *Sound Currency*, II). A number of States used the principle of bond security without adopting general incorporation; e.g., Virginia (*Acts* 1852–53, p. 77; *Journal of Political Economy*, XXXVI, pp. 480–85); and Kentucky (*Laws* 1851, chap. 631). The principle was strongly favored in South Carolina by Memminger and was under active discussion in Maryland, where a bill was defeated, however, in 1852. (A. C. Bryan, 'History of State Banking in Maryland,' in Johns Hopkins University *Studies*, 1899, XVII.)

troller the right of requiring an additional deposit when notes fell below par.

Another defect uncovered by New York experience was in the use of real estate mortgages as a basis of issue. Here the defect was again not so much a defect in ultimate sufficiency as in immediate availability; for mortgages were subject to a tedious foreclosure process and land values usually fell sharply in periods of financial stress. The prior experience with land as a basis of paper money had been disastrous — in the eighteenth-century 'bubbles,' the French assignats, the Colonial Land Bank of Massachusetts, and the land banks of the Cotton South. The problem was, however, no easy one. Such a level-headed man as Benjamin Franklin was disposed to regard the traditional stability of land as a sound basis. Even Alexander Hamilton, in his early years, looked favorably upon the land-security idea; but, in his discussion of the proposed United States Bank in 1790, he gave the classic arguments against it.[1] There was, however, a real need for agricultural credit, and it should not be regarded as strange that a nation of farmers, faced with the development of a great expanse of cheap land, should attempt to coin it into money. The reluctance of sound bankers to extend loans or base a circulation on such frozen assets explains in part the recurrent farmer suspicion of bankers. If the banker chose either horn of the dilemma, his popularity was not enhanced. The experience of New York with mortgage security was so unsatisfactory that Millard Fillmore, as Comptroller, advised its abandonment. Robert Dale Owen, whom none could accuse of being impervious to social sympathy, pressed the same view in Indiana. On the basis of this experience, therefore, the National Banking System did not allow real estate to be used as a basis for notes or as security for loans.

The problem of agricultural credit, however, was not solved by its abandonment. Before the Civil War this matter was most constructively approached in New Orleans, where a distinction was made between loans from capital, and loans from deposits. Capital loans, called 'dead weight,' might be made on real estate, but demand deposits, called

[1] Miller, p. 130.

'the bank movement,' could only be loaned on short paper 'moving in a rapid circle.' The proscription of agricultural credit by the National System is a partial explanation of the hostility in the West toward National banks, and the striking growth of State banks permitted to loan on mortgages, as well as the greater number of State bank failures in periods of depression. The problem remained a major one of National finance for fifty years after the establishment of the National System. Under the Federal Reserve System, National banks were permitted to extend loans on real estate, subject to careful regulations. The Farm Loan Act, however, was designed to divert agricultural credit to safer channels than commercial banking. National banks under the Federal Reserve System, however, have availed themselves very cautiously of this privilege of real estate loans, which no doubt explains the smaller number of failures in recent years among them as compared to smaller State banks in the agricultural communities.

Another defect of a bond-secured note issue was an inherent inelasticity. This had been noted in the New York system in the fifties when, in a period of a rising business cycle, capital was attracted to more productive investment than the purchase of bonds upon which to issue paper money. This problem was not solved in the period before the Civil War — although the defect was temporarily eased by the use of clearing-house certificates. Secretary Chase was aware of the problem, but suggested that it was for the future to solve. It engaged the attention of financiers and economists for years during the currency-reform discussion which preceded the establishment of the Federal Reserve System. President Wilson had this in mind when he referred to our 'banking and currency system based on the necessity of the Government to sell its bonds fifty years ago, and perfectly adapted to concentrating cash and restricting credit.' The new system has been made more 'elastically responsive to sound credit' by the use of ordinary commercial securities. The merits of the principle of a bond-secured note issue belong to the field of technical finance, and it is sufficient to emphasize in this discussion that the principle was a product of State experience.

LEGAL RESERVES

(a) *Circulation*

The principle of a legal minimum reserve against circulation was first effectively applied in Louisiana in 1842. It was, of course, regarded as good practice to maintain such a reserve and the most conservative bankers of America followed the practice of the Bank of England announced in 1832. But the temptation was great and the rule, not generally understood, was more violated than observed. The almost universal suspension of specie payments in the panic of 1837 was the occasion of widespread discussion and constructive legislation. The New York law of 1838 required a twelve and one half per cent reserve, but this was repealed in 1840. The collapse of the land and property banks of Louisiana brought forth a strong anti-bank movement and, at the same time, constructive legislation. The principles adopted were largely those advised by Edmund J. Forstall, a prominent sugar planter, historian, and banker of New Orleans. In 1837 he formulated a plan for a thirty-three and one third per cent reserve against both circulation and deposits. This system was adopted in 1842 and until the Civil War gave Louisiana a National reputation for sound finance, but until the panic of 1857 found few imitators. A reform movement in Ohio resulted in a law of 1845 requiring a thirty per cent reserve and the Indiana free-bank law of 1852 fixed the reserve at twelve and one half per cent.

The panic of 1857, which New Orleans weathered without suspensions, directed general attention to her system and resulted in several State reserve laws. Missouri in 1857 required thirty-three and one third per cent; Iowa, in 1858, twenty-five per cent; and Minnesota in 1858, twenty per cent. Aside from the facts that there was a growing appreciation of the need of such laws and a definite movement to enact them, the fact that Samuel Hooper, of Massachusetts, and Amasa Walker succeeded in pushing through a reserve law is significant. Samuel Hooper, much impressed by Louisiana experience, brought to the task of preparing a National System a keen sense of the value of reserves. Moreover, it is a point worthy of notice that these reserve laws

were enacted in States where the hard-money attitude had
been particularly strong.   In Louisiana, for instance, a constitution of 1845 abolished credit paper; in Missouri a constitution of 1845 (adopted in convention, but defeated in
referendum) had prohibited bank paper; and Iowa had for
twenty years permitted no paper money.   Furthermore,
Amasa Walker, who helped to write the Massachusetts law
of 1858, was the most prominent American economist defending Benton's theory, and Chase in recommending a National System could not avoid showing his hard-money background.

(b) Deposits

There was little recognition of the need of any protection
for deposits prior to 1857.   A very general ideal prevailed
that a depositor was a voluntary creditor and, therefore, entitled to no protection beyond the general assets of the bank.
The New York Bank Commissioners in 1841 said: 'No man
is bound to deposit in a bank unless he pleases, and...no
good reason can be perceived why he should be entitled to
greater security than that of the bank to which he gives
credit.'   The safety-fund of New York was applied to the
protection of deposits as well as notes, and the Louisiana
law of 1842 required a thirty-three and one third per cent
reserve against total liability, which, of course, included deposits.   During the fifties, however, bank deposits became a
very important item and in the case of panic constituted a
threat no less dangerous than circulation.   The panic of 1857
was a depositors' run no less than a bill-holders' and forced
general consideration of the question.   The importance of deposits was noted by George Tucker, the economist; Governor
Chase, of Ohio; and George Opdyke, of New York.   The
message of Governor King, of New York, January 6, 1858,
declared that the panic had been due to deposits rather than
circulation.   He proposed a law requiring a twenty-five per
cent deposit reserve, saying: 'Under a law similar to this, the
chief banks of New Orleans, above all banks of the country,
were enabled to resist the pressure of universal suspension
elsewhere and maintain their integrity.' [1]   The Iowa law of

[1] 35th Cong., 1st Sess., *House Ex. Doc.* No. 107, pp. 157-59.

1858 required a twenty-five per cent, and the Massachusetts law a fifteen per cent reserve; but the principle appears to have found no imitation elsewhere.

INDIVIDUAL STOCKHOLDER LIABILITY

The principle of individual stockholder liability — that is, liability in his individual capacity in addition to the amount invested — did not receive general recognition in banking legislation prior to 1850. It was applied in isolated instances before 1837, but first came to be widely discussed as a reform measure after the panic of 1837. It was adopted by New York in 1846 (effective January 1, 1850), and came quite generally to be required by the new Jacksonian constitutions of the fifties. The standard type required liability to an amount equal to the shares owned, in addition to such shares; the identical provision of the National Bank Law.[1] This principle was not derived from the Second Bank. Benton quite cogently pointed out, in 1831, the absence of this principle;[2] and the Governor of Missouri, no doubt under Benton's influence, attempted to secure it as a provision of the charter of the State Bank of Missouri. Neither Michigan nor Florida in bitter anti-bank mood after the panic of 1837 was prepared for the full principle applied to the normal hazards of business. Michigan in 1839 applied it in case of fraud,[3] and Florida, by her Constitution of 1839, applied it 'when an act of forfeiture is committed.[4] The New York

[1] Davis R. Dewey, 'State Banking Before the Civil War,' in National Monetary Commission *Reports*, IV (1910), pp. 117–20. Earlier forms of liability, such as those of New York in 1827, and Indiana in 1834, made it effective only in case of fraudulent insolvency rather than for the normal hazards of business. John Brough, of Ohio, in a report, January 11, 1839, advocated individual liability in cases of issue beyond three hundred per cent of specie reserve. He cited instances from laws of Massachusetts, New York, and Rhode Island. Condy Raguet, in *Currency and Banking* (1839), p. 109, favored some form of individual liability, but was skeptical of its adoption.

[2] *Abridgment of Debates*, XI, p. 155, February 2, 1831.

[3] Michigan *Laws* (1839), pp. 57–58. The Michigan general law of March 15, 1837, applied unlimited liability to both directors and stockholders, but this clause was made ineffective by court decisions.

[4] Thorpe, II, pp. 678–79. The clause also said, rather ambiguously, 'or when it is dissolved or expires.'

law of 1846 appears to have been the model for subsequent legislation.

The development of this principle, as well as that of freedom of incorporation, must be considered in relation to the growth of the corporation as a form of business association. The corporation had, of course, long been used, particularly for churches, schools, and trading companies; but ordinary business in the Jacksonian era was still conducted largely by individuals and partnerships. The United States Bank, with its $35,000,000 of capital and many branches, was a 'monster' in the eyes of that generation. The corporation, however, possessed many advantages, and responding to the drive of new economic forces, showed a particularly active growth. The first important legal discussion of the corporation in America was Angell and Ames, *Law of Private Corporations* (1831); and the *American Jurist*, reviewing this treatise, called attention to the growing importance of the subject. With the Federal Government refusing aid for internal improvement and withdrawing from banking, and with State credit exhausted, the problem of economic development was too large for individual enterprise. Associated capital was inevitable, and the private corporation was the answer. American business merely passed from the individual to the corporation much as in the period after the Civil War it tended to pass from small corporations to large trusts and mergers.[1]

This economic transition, however, was not accomplished without suspicion and opposition. In the first place, it clearly ran counter to the agrarian individualism of the period, and a fear arose that in some manner 'republican institutions' were menaced. Constitutional conventions seriously debated and sometimes enacted proposals to prohibit corporations in competition with individual enterprise. The phrase 'soulless corporation' was born and began its long career. This arose from the fear that an individual in an association lost his natural sense of sympathy and responsibility. 'Individuals,' said Senator McDuffie, of South Carolina, 'are always open to impressions of generosity. But classes... and sections... being destitute like corporations,

[1] C. R. Fish, *Rise of the Common Man* (New York, 1927), pp. 50–61.

of individual responsibility, are like them, destitute of hearts and souls.' There were, moreover, certain legal developments which increased suspicion. By common law individuals in partnerships were liable in full for their obligations. By a fiction of American courts, however, the corporation was endowed with 'personality.' The corporate 'person,' therefore, was liable for its obligations to the extent of its assets; but the individual in the corporation was exempted from any liability beyond his investment. This was clearly a natural exemption, designed to attract capital, but in period of financial stress it appeared to many men holding the notes of insolvent banks that stockholders were given unjust exemption. This idea was deepened with the passage of the National Bankruptcy Law. Anti-corporation sentiment was strengthened by certain legal maxims of John Marshall which sanctioned the doctrine of 'perpetuity' of charters. It appeared to many persons, therefore, that a corporation with an inviolable charter granted by special act, lacking a sense of individual responsibility, having recourse to bankruptcy, and stifling individual enterprise, was an omen fraught with danger — another privilege against which suspicion ran in deep currents.

Here again was a problem to solve, rather than a natural phenomenon to destroy. In approaching it there was a strong tendency in some quarters to make stockholder liability as full as in a partnership. The Iowa Convention of 1844 wrote this principle into the Constitution, and a motion to substitute limited liability lost by a vote of 46 to 20. Governor French, of Illinois, in 1851 vetoed a general bank law for the reason that it lacked unlimited liability. Missouri, in her unratified Constitution of 1845, required unlimited liability for all corporations. The West, in thinking on this matter, however, always had the afterthought of railroads; and although such corporations were allowed, they rarely lived in peace. The standard method, however, for banks was to require the limited liability of the New York type. The reservation of the right to repeal or amend any charter granted was especially frequent in the anti-corporation constitutions of the West — a principle which passed into the National Bank Act along with limited liability.

CHAPTER VIII

POST–BELLUM INFLUENCE OF EARLY EXPERIENCE

MANY principles and attitudes which developed in the experience summarized in the preceding chapter have continued to exert an enduring influence in the period since the Civil War. This is shown in amendments to the National Bank Act, in reform discussions following panics, and in State bank legislation. This chapter, while making no effort at an exhaustive analysis, will briefly summarize some of this influence.

Various amendments to the National Bank Act show the influence of early experience. The original act of February 25, 1863, was recast by an act of June 3, 1864. Among the important changes made were: (1) ten per cent of the net profits must be carried to a surplus fund until it was equal to twenty per cent of the capital; (2) par redemption must be provided at New York City and other important commercial centers; and (3) National banks must not loan on real estate.[1] The requirement of a surplus was similar to that required in the State Bank of Indiana, par redemption had been provided for in the New England Suffolk System and New York law; and the proscription of real estate loans was a result of adverse experience with that type of loan discussed elsewhere. By an act of June 20, 1874, the original requirement of a reserve against notes was repealed, and at the same time a five per cent 'redemption fund' was set up. This was contributed by member

---

[1] A. T. Huntington and R. J. Mawhinney, *Laws of the United States Concerning Money, Banking and Loans, 1778–1909*, in National Monetary Commission *Reports*, p. 361. It should be noted that in this final chapter organic continuity is frequently inferred from similarity of principle — not always a safe conclusion. No systematic attempt is made, moreover, to carry the discussion beyond the studies of the National Monetary Commission. The author is primarily concerned with the question of historical continuity rather than with the merits of technical principles or their practical application.

banks and held by the Treasury Department in a manner somewhat like that of the New York safety-fund, but was, of course, essentially different from the New York fund in that there was no mutual guaranty involved.[1]

For several years after the establishment of the National Banking System, criticism was directed against the limitation of $300,000,000 placed on the total amount of circulation. This, it was asserted, was a violation of the New York principle of free banking and constituted a monopoly. Silas M. Stilwell, one of the alleged authors of the National Bank Act, maintained that the new system was different from its New York model in this respect — the former restricting the quantity, the latter regulating the quality of circulation.[2] Henry C. Carey, a prominent economist, held much the same views, and in a series of public letters addressed to President Grant, denounced the new system as sectional rather than National. According to his figures, the Eastern States in 1860 had $73,000,000 of bank circulation; but under the new system they had $173,000,000. In the rest of the Nation, he asserted, circulation had been reduced in the same period from $134,000,000 to $124,000,-000. He insisted, moreover, that the currency of New York City was three hundred and fifty per cent what it was in 1860, that of Boston three hundred and forty per cent, and that of Philadelphia three hundred and sixty per cent. This, he thought, constituted 'a monopoly of money power without parallel in the world.'[3] The most serious opposition came from the rising greenback movement. So threatening did this become after 1867 that the new system, according to Hepburn, 'suffered a precarious existence for the next ten years with strong probabilities of its abolition.'[4] The

[1] Huntington and Mawhinney, op. cit. Section 16 of the Federal Reserve Act retained the principle of a redemption fund.

[2] A Report of Two Interviews with the Honorable Silas M. Stilwell (Chicago, 1874).

[3] Henry C. Carey, Prospect of the Currency (Philadelphia, 1868).

[4] A. B. Hepburn, Contest for Sound Money (New York, 1903), p. 328; a notable treatise by a former Comptroller of the Currency, and a man prominent in the currency discussions of the period. His book is dedicated to Alexander Hamilton, and on the technical side is no doubt sound enough. When he attempts historical interpretation, however,

limitation on the currency was removed by the Resumption Act of January 14, 1875, and 'free banking' permitted. No great increase in National circulation resulted, however, for in the rising business cycle after the panic of 1873, capital was attracted away from bond investment as a basis of note issue. Nevertheless, says Hepburn, 'although bank organization and the issue of bank currency was now absolutely free, the cry of monopoly was still maintained.'

The more serious political attacks on the system subsided by 1880 and the economic argument on its defects began. The inelastic nature of the bond-secured note issue became a practical problem in the eighties and began to attract the attention of economists and financiers. In the financial stringency of 1882 the situation was temporarily eased by the use of clearing-house certificates. Henry W. Cannon, Comptroller of the Currency, in 1884 recommended the adoption of the safety-fund principle of security — 'a guarantee fund to be accumulated from the tax on circulation, the gain on lost notes, and the interest on the redemption fund.' In 1890, Canada, which had tried the bond-security principle and found it defective, adopted the safety-fund. In 1892, the National platform of the Democratic Party advocated the repeal of the ten-per-cent tax on State bank notes, but this proposal fortunately was not adopted.

The panic of 1893 started a period of discussion on cur-

he is apt to be a bit dogmatic. Two of the leaders of this movement to repeal the National System were George H. Pendleton and William Allen, of Ohio. The former was elected Governor of Ohio in 1867 with a platform advocating repeal, and the movement became known as the 'Ohio Idea.' Allen, curiously enough, was a former hard-money Jacksonian Democrat — so intimate a friend of Andrew Jackson, indeed, that he was one of the select group which met at the home of the Blairs in Washington in March, 1837, to hear Jackson's final words of advice. One wonders what attitude Thomas Hart Benton would have taken in the new period. The soft-money movement in the West following so close on the heels of the hard-money movement is one of the most amazing enigmas of American financial history. Illinois, for example, turned almost immediately from writing the hard-money Constitution of 1862 to demanding greenbacks. It has never been a thesis of historians that consistency rules the world, but it has been the view that such complete reversals seldom occur.

rency reform which became increasingly more fertile in the years preceding the passing of the Federal Reserve Act. The period from 1893 to 1913, in fact, reminds one of the creative age following the panic of 1837. In 1894, the American Bankers' Association proposed an elaborate reorganization — the Baltimore Plan — including the use of a five-per-cent guaranty fund. Secretary of the Treasury Lyman Gage, in 1897, and the Indianapolis Monetary Convention of 1898 proposed the abrogation of the bond-security principle and the use of a safety-fund. Secretary Gage in 1900 renewed his recommendation for a safety-fund and 'suggested a federated system or federated bank somewhat analogous to the general Government and the States.' The law of 1900 made it easier to organize National banks, and various factors, including the gold discoveries of the Klondike, helped to ease the situation in the early years of the century. The panic of 1907, however, renewed discussion of currency reform and some active steps were taken in that direction. The Aldrich-Vreeland Act of 1908 gave partial relief, and the National Monetary Commission was created to make exhaustive studies of banking. The report of the Commission was made early in 1912 and advocated a central bank somewhat like the Second United States Bank. When this Aldrich Plan was presented, debate developed some of the acrimony of 1832. Senator Aldrich, Chairman of the Commission, was as anathema to the western Insurgents and Democrats of 1912 as Nicholas Biddle had been to the Jacksonian Democrats eighty year. before. He had been prominent in the Senate for thirty years, was widely known as an advocate of high protection, and generally regarded as closely identified with 'big business' — at that time a burning issue of politics. The Federal Reserve System of 1913 cannot be regarded as a restoration of the Second United States Bank, any more than was the National Banking System of 1863. Much water had gone under the bridge since that hot July day in 1832 when an angry Andrew Jackson vetoed the charter of the 'Monster,' but by the testimony of Senator Carter Glass, the ghost of the General still stalked the streets of Washington in 1913.

State bank legislation in the period since the establishment of the National Banking System offers another field
for the study of the continuity of influence. The National
Bank Act, by placing a ten-per-cent tax on State bank notes,
in effect deprived State banks of their note-issue function.
As banks of discount and deposit, however, they have continued to exist and grow under State regulation. For several
years after the Civil War, there were fewer State banks
than National, but by the turn of the century, the National
banks were outnumbered. In 1909, there were in the
United States 11,292 State banks and 6893 National. The
relative capital, while less impressive, nevertheless showed
a remarkable State bank growth — from one sixth of the
total bank capital of the Nation in 1879 to nearly one half
in 1909. The principal growth had occurred in the South
and West. In 1910, only two per cent of New England bank
capital was under State regulation; in the South it was
eighty per cent.[1]

The principle of general or free incorporation, which constituted one of the most important developments of the
early systems, has worked its way since the Civil War to
almost Nation-wide adoption. The West, which formerly
had shown a strong partiality for this method, continued to
lead in the movement. Each new State, without exception,
adopted the principle in its constitution: Nevada (1864);
Nebraska (1866); Colorado (1876); the Omnibus States of
1889 — North Dakota, South Dakota, Montana, Wyoming,
Washington, and Idaho; Utah (1895); and Oklahoma (1907).
Other western States, which formerly had permitted incorporation by either general or special act, tended to adopt
general incorporation as the exclusive method. Elsewhere
the immediate tendency was to revert 'to the exclusive use
of special charters for the incorporation of banks.' In New
England special charters were generally followed until the
end of the century — the *ante-bellum* free-bank laws of
Massachusetts, Vermont, and Connecticut remaining dead

[1] George E. Barnett, 'State Banks and Trust Companies,' in National
Monetary Commission *Reports* (1911) — an expansion of an earlier
study, 'State Banking in the United States Since the Passage of the
National Bank Act,' in Johns Hopkins University *Studies*, XX (1902).

letters. New York retained her free-bank law, except for trust companies — the latter being included, however, in 1887. Pennsylvania and New Jersey retained their early free-bank laws; but general incorporation as the exclusive method was not adopted in the former until 1873, and in the latter not until 1875. By 1910, however, all States of the East, except Delaware and Maryland, had adopted general incorporation. The Delaware Constitution of 1897 expressly excluded banks and trust companies from the general law. In the South the movement is also discernible. Louisiana, alone of the southern States before the Civil War, had prohibited special incorporation by her Constitution of 1845. During the Reconstruction period and subsequently, each southern State, except North Carolina, adopted general incorporation as the exclusive method. In 1903, North Carolina adopted a general law applying to banks and trust companies, but special charters might still be granted. By 1910, so general had the movement become that special charters for banks were possible in only three States — Maryland, Delaware, and North Carolina; and in Delaware alone was special incorporation the exclusive method.

The anti-bank attitudes of the Mississippi Valley and the Pacific Coast persisted into the later period. Texas, which by her Jacksonian Constitution of 1845 had prohibited corporate banks, adhered to that policy for sixty years. The restriction of 1845 was renewed in the Constitutions of 1861 and 1866. The Reconstruction Constitution of 1868, which did not represent the mood of Texas, temporarily removed the restriction; but the Constitution of 1875 restored the prohibition of 1845. It was not until November, 1904, that an amendment was adopted by popular referendum authorizing bank corporations, and the following year a general bank law was passed. Moreover, as will be seen later, Texas was in a mood after the panic of 1907 to enact strict banking regulations. Private banks, of course, continued to exist throughout the period from 1845 to 1905. The hard-money Constitution of Oregon in 1857 had prohibited banks; but the State Supreme Court held that the provision applied only to banks of issue, which in any case had been taxed out of existence by National law. The California hard-money attitudes persisted into the later period, and even the National System was unpopular for many years. Pitt Cooke, who was sent by his brother Jay to San Francisco to sell post-war bonds, made little progress because the interest was payable in 'lawful money.'[1] The Pacific Coast for many years, in fact, showed a remarkable partiality for hard money. Various provisions, which had been adopted in western constitutions of the early period, continued to obstruct the process of banking legislation. The elaborate referendum process was held by the courts of Missouri, Kansas, Iowa, and Ohio to apply only to banks of issue; but in Michigan, Illinois, and Wisconsin it was held to apply also to banks of discount and deposit. The referendum requirement was removed in Wisconsin in 1902, and in Michigan in 1908; but it still held in Illinois in 1910. The requirement of a two-thirds vote of the Legislature for bank charters still held in Minnesota in 1910, and was substituted for the referendum process in Wisconsin and Michigan in 1902 and 1908.

Another test of continuity of influence is the tendency toward individual stockholder liability in banking legislation. As shown by preceding chapters, State experience by 1860 had arrived in the main at the principle of individual liability; that is, liability for an amount equal to the par value of stock owned in addition to the stock — sometimes called double liability or statutory liability. This liability, however, ran in most cases against the issue obligation of banks. With the suppression of State banks of issue, the question thereafter was whether statutory liability should be applied for the deposit obligation. Many variations and mutations developed in the different States, but the parent stem of all the legislation was the early bank laws. In some States li-

---

[1] E. P. Oberholtzer, *Jay Cooke, Financier*, I, pp. 629–34, W. C. Ralston, Cashier of the Bank of California to Pitt Cooke, July 1, 1865. The State Convention of the Democratic Party in 1865 resolved that 'The whole history of California is a triumphant vindication of her State policy of a gold and silver circulating medium....' The Union Convention of the same year rejected a resolution favoring the National Banking System. It was not, in fact, until 1870 that a National bank was established in California — The National Gold Bank of San Francisco. (W. J. Davis, *Political Conventions of California*, pp. 221–22; 225.)

ability was applied by constitutional provision for unpaid stock subscription only, and in nine States and Territories no provision was made for additional liability. In more than half of the States, however, individual liability was imposed either by the State Constitution or by statute. In all cases, except two, the liability was double — in California it was unlimited, and in Colorado it was triple. In three States it was for the benefit of depositors only, and in all but five it was applied to both banks and trust companies. The liability in most cases was proportionate — 'equally and ratably and not one for another.' [1] In a few cases it was mutual — 'jointly and for each other.' Professor Barnett, the closest student of State banking since the Civil War, thinks that the principle 'has not been of great service as a protection to bank creditors against loss.' This has been due, he thinks, to enforcement difficulties — transfers of stock and court decisions making the liability secondary rather than primary.

Reserves against deposits had received little recognition in the early banking systems. The New York Safety-Fund System, and the Louisiana and Iowa systems had adopted the principle, and the depositor panic of 1857 had occasioned a wide discussion of the matter, which led to its adoption into the National Bank Act. It was not, however, until the great growth of State banks in the eighties that anything like a general movement in this direction occurred. The States of Connecticut, Ohio, and Minnesota by 1881 had adopted reserves ranging from ten to twenty per cent; and by 1910 a reserve of some kind was required in all except ten States. A distinct tendency developed in State legislation to distinguish between demand and time deposits; and either require against the latter no reserves whatever, or a smaller amount than for demand deposits. The reserves in many cases might consist of bonds. An interesting development was the movement in the West after the panic of 1907 to protect deposits

[1] The National Bank Act of June 3, 1864, which superseded the original act of February 25, 1863, used the same words. Section 2 of the Federal Reserve Act of December 23, 1913, held shareholders 'individually responsible, equally and ratably, and not one for another... to the extent of the amount of their subscription to such stock at par value thereof in addition to the amount subscribed.'

by a so-called guaranty fund. Beginning in the new State of Oklahoma by a law of December 17, 1907; the movement was endorsed by the National platform of the Democratic Party in 1908, and spread by 1909 into the old anti-bank State of Texas and the populist States of Kansas, Nebraska, and South Dakota. This principle had been under discussion in these States since the panic of 1893, and may be viewed as resulting from the panics and the resurgent anti-bank reactions they engendered.[1]

Differences of policy and practice between National and State bank systems developed in the matter of permitting loans on real estate. National banks had been forbidden to loan on mortgage collateral, but State banks and trust companies have generally been permitted this type of loan. One of the clearest principles evolved by early State experience was that real estate offered poor security for bank notes and deposits. The policy of some States in this matter, therefore, would seem to have run counter to sound theory and experience. It may be ventured that the explanation lies partly in the fact that State banks established in agricultural communities permitted real estate loans from necessity, or what was regarded as such, and possibly also to enable them to compete more effectively with the National banks. State' legislation, however, did not ignore the problems of agricultural credit. Regulations of various kinds were devised; including a limit on the aggregate amount of real estate loans, requiring two thirds director votes, taking a loan at a fifty-per-cent valuation of the property, distinguishing between demand and time deposits, requiring first mortgages rather than second, and making a distinction between loans made in agricultural and commercial communities.

The National Monetary Commission recognized the problem and reported that 'the provision that National banks shall not make loans on real estate restricts their power to serve farmers and other borrowers in rural communities.' The Federal Reserve Act of 1913 permitted limited lending on improved and unencumbered farm lands, and an amendment in 1916 somewhat further liberalized the provisions

[1] Thornton Cooke, 'The Insurance of Bank Deposits in the West,' an appendix to Barnett, *State Banks and Trust Companies*.

regulating real estate loans. Under specific limitations imposed, the Act has accordingly permitted some modification of the traditional practice of the National Banking System.[1]

This study has traced the emergence of the National Banking System from the early experience of the American States in the quarter-century following the fall of the Second United States Bank. Some attempt has been made, moreover, to show the later influence on State and National legislation of the principles evolved in early State experience. It is a record of principles developed by States and tested in the laboratory of their experience before National adoption. Altogether it testifies to the remarkable creative power of States under a Federal System, to the constructive character of the Jacksonian era in finance, and to the continuity of American financial institutions.

[1] *Report of the National Monetary Commission*, January 9, 1912. Section 24 of the Federal Reserve Act provided that any National bank outside of the three central reserve cities of New York, Chicago, and St. Louis (the latter ceased to be a central reserve city in 1922), might 'make loans secured by improved and unencumbered farm lands, situated within its Federal Reserve District, but no such loan shall be made for a longer time than five years, nor for any amount exceeding fifty percentum of the actual value of the property offered as security....' Such loans were limited in the aggregate amount to twenty-five per cent of the capital and surplus of the bank or to one third of its time deposits. The amendment of 1916 extended to banks the privilege of lending on improved and unencumbered property other than farm land, such loans being included within the limitations noted as to amount, and being restricted to a one-year term.

BIBLIOGRAPHICAL NOTE

BIBLIOGRAPHICAL NOTE

GENERAL ACCOUNTS

I. SECONDARY STUDIES

1. Dewey, Davis Rich: 'State Banking Before the Civil War,' in National Monetary Commission *Reports*, V (1910); a valuable work by a well-known student of financial history tracing the evolution of the technical aspects of banking without intending to relate them to particular States or to the historical currents of the period.

2. Miller, H. E.: 'Banking Theories in the United States Before 1860,' in Harvard Economic *Studies*, XXX (1928); a careful analysis of theory as reflected in contemporary pamphlets and works on economics.

II. CONTEMPORARY WORKS

1. Gouge, William: *Short History of Paper Money* (Philadelphia, 1833). This book was written by a lifelong advocate of hard money and presents a dark picture of the attempts to use credit paper. It was published in London by William Cobbett under the title of *The Curse of Paper Money*. Cobbett agreed with the thesis, but was irritated by the style.

2. Raguet, Condy: *Currency and Banking* (Philadelphia, 1839); by a prominent advocate of credit money under the New York free-bank principle.

3. Gallatin, Albert: *Suggestions on the Currency* (New York, 1841); contains concise analyses of the Safety-Fund and Free-Bank Systems of New York.

4. Tucker, George: *Theory of Banks and Money Investigated* (Boston, 1839); by a defender of credit money under the English-New Orleans principle of specie reserves.

5. Walker, Amasa: *Nature and Uses of Money and Mixed Currency* (Boston, 1857); an argument for hard money by a veteran economist.

SPECIAL ACCOUNTS

I. SECONDARY STUDIES.
Special accounts include a wide variety of material of varying importance. In general they are apt to

lack perspective, to emphasize the personal and picturesque, and to be engaged in digging masses of undigested facts out of one place and burying them in another. Such material has been of slight value, but has been cited at appropriate points. A few critical monographs have been produced, however, and these have been of great assistance. They include:

1. Cable, John Ray: 'The Missouri State Bank,' in Columbia University *Studies*, CII (1923).

2. Chaddock, R. E.: 'The Safety-Fund Banking System of New York,' in National Monetary Commission *Reports*, IV (1910); one of a series of important studies produced during the discussions preceding the Federal Reserve Act.

3. Cole, A. C.: *The Era of the Civil War* (Springfield, 1919); a volume of the Centennial History of Illinois and especially valuable for banking in Illinois during the fifties.

4. Davis, A. M.: 'The Origins of the National Banking System,' in National Monetary Commission *Reports*, V (1910); deals largely with the immediate origins.

5. Esarey, Logan: *State Banking in Indiana: 1814–1873*; misunderstands the 'free-bank' movement.

6. Harding, W. F.: 'The State Bank of Indiana,' in *Journal of Political Economy*, IV (1895); contains text of the charter and statistics of experience, a careful study of a powerful State bank.

7. Merk, Frederick: *Economic History of Wisconsin During the Civil War Decade* (Madison, 1916); important for the effect of the Civil War on the Wisconsin currency.

8. Pease, T. C.: *The Frontier State* (Springfield, 1918); another volume of the Illinois Centennial History and of value for banking in the forties.

9. Preston, H. O.: *History of Banking in Iowa.* Iowa City, 1922.

10. Scott, W. A. *Repudiation of State Debts* (New York, 1893); a prize essay by an eminent student of banking.

II. CONTEMPORARY WORKS

1. Adams, C. F.: *Further Reflections on the Currency.* Boston, 1837.

2. Appleton, Nathan: *Remarks on Currency and Banking.* Boston, 1841.

3. Gouge, William: *Fiscal History of Texas.* Philadelphia, 1852.

4. Hooper, Samuel: *An Examination of the Theory and Effect of Laws Regulating the Amount of Specie in Banks.* Boston, 1860.

5. Trotter, Alexander: *Observations on the Financial Position and Credit of Such States of the North American Union as have Contracted Public Debts.* London, 1839.

6. Tucker, George: 'Banks or No Banks,' in *Hunt's Merchants' Magazine,* XXXVIII (1858).

COLLECTIONS OF DOCUMENTS

I. GOVERNMENT DOCUMENTS

1. *Reports of the Secretary of the Treasury on the Condition of State Banks in the Union.* These reports were made pursuant to a resolution of the House July 10, 1832, directing the Secretary to collect information on State banks. They constitute a rich vein of information, consisting of documents forwarded by every State and Territory of the Union, together with statistics compiled by the Treasury Department. They were collected under Democratic auspices from 1832 to 1841, when they were discontinued during the Harrison-Tyler period. R. J. Walker, Secretary of Treasury under Polk, resumed the publication, and, attempting to fill in the gap since 1841, made the most valuable and voluminous report in 1846. Succeeding Secretaries continued the reports until the adoption of the National Banking System. They become less valuable in the fifties, however, and after 1861 contain little data on the South. Altogether, this series of reports constitutes the principal source of this study. They are printed in House Executive Documents as follows:

Congress	Session	Number of Document	Congress	Session	Number of Document
24	2	65	32	2	66
25	2	79	33	1	102
25	3	227	33	2	82
26	1	172	34	1	102
26	2	111	34	3	87
29	1	226	35	1	107
29	2	120	36	1	49
30	1	77	37	3	25
31	1	68	38	1	20
32	1	122			

2. Other Treasury Department material has been consulted, such as Annual Reports, and Reports on special subjects called for by the Senate and House; e.g., banking in Wisconsin Territory. These consist of:

24th Cong., 1st Sess., House Ex. Doc. No. 146
24th Cong., 2d Sess., House Ex. Doc. No. 2
25th Cong., 2d Sess., House Ex. Doc. No. 193
25th Cong., 2d Sess., House Ex. Doc. No. 262
25th Cong., 3d Sess., House Ex. Doc. No. 232
24th Cong., 2d Sess., Senate Doc. No. 2
25th Cong. 2d Sess., Senate Doc. No. 471

3. *Tenth Census*, VII (1880), 'A History of State Debts.'

II. STATE DOCUMENTS. No systematic attempt has been made to study the documents of each State for material relating to banking. At particular points, however, where the Federal documents have seemed inadequate, recourse has been had to State material. Altogether, this has amounted to a large number of documents consulted, but to list each particular one would tend to magnify unduly their importance as a source for this study. State statutes have been used for the laws and charters of the ¬rincipal banking systems established in the period. Legislative documents ordinarily contain the regular reports of administrative officers charged with banking supervision; e.g., Comptroller of Currency, Superintendent of Banking, Board of Currency, Bank Commissioners, Auditor, or Treasurer; and, also the reports of standing Committees on Banks and the reports of special committees of investigation following the panic of 1837. Legislative Journals frequently contain Governors' messages as well as committee reports. For the States of Massachusetts, New York, Ohio, and Illinois comprehensive guides were available: A. R. Hasse, *An Index to the Economic Materials Contained in State Documents*. In the case of South Carolina the collected documents — *Resolutions and Reports* — have been used almost exclusively. The no-bank movement of the Mississippi Valley is reflected in the debates of the various constitutional conventions of the fifties, and the final bank clauses are found in Thorpe's standard compilation, *Federal and State Constitutions*. Governors' messages, which frequently throw light on the problem, have been published separately with biographical introductions for the States of Michigan and Missouri. The *Court Reports* of Mississippi were used in connection with the repudiation movement of that State. Altogether, the most important State documents consulted were the constitutional convention debates as follows:

1. California: *Debates in the Convention of California*. Washington, 1850.

2. Illinois: *Convention Journal* (Springfield, 1847); and, *Convention Journal* (Springfield, 1862).

3. Indiana: *Report of the Debates and Proceedings*. Indianapolis, 1850.

4. Iowa: *Fragments of the Debates of the Iowa Conventions 1844 and 1846* (edited by B. F. Shambaugh, Iowa City, 1900); and *Official Report of the Debates and Proceedings of the Convention of 1857* (Davenport, 1857).

5. Louisiana: *Proceedings and Debates of the Convention of Louisiana*. New Orleans, 1845.

6. Missouri: *Journal of the Convention of the State of Missouri.* Jefferson City, 1845.

7. New York: *Convention Journal*. New York, 1846.

8. Nevada: *Debates and Proceedings of the Constitutional Convention of Nevada*. Carson City, 1864.

9. Ohio: *Official Report of the Debates and Proceedings of the Ohio State Convention*. Columbus, 1851.

10. Wisconsin: *Convention of 1846* (edited by Milo M. Quaife), in *Wisconsin Historical Collections*, XXVII; and *Journal of the Convention to Form a Constitution for the State of Wisconsin*. Madison, 1848.

III. PERIODICALS, ETC.

1. The most important periodical consulted was: *The Bankers' Magazine and Statistical Register* — cited *Bankers' Magazine* — which began under the editorship of J. Smith Homans in New York in 1846. It has a wealth of statistical material, ordinarily published the more important laws passed, and contains articles of merit by contemporary financiers. Second in importance is *Hunt's Merchants' Magazine*. *De Bow's Review* has little of value on banking. *Sound Currency* was not a contemporary periodical, but a temporary publication of the period following the panic of 1893. It was edited by L. Carroll Root, financier of New York and New Orleans; and besides articles by the editor, contains many studies by Horace White and others. The articles, although of much value, are apt to be very posi-

tive about 'Sound Currency,' to repudiate the inelastic bond-secured currency, and to carry that prejudice back into the *ante-bellum* period.

2. Newspapers have been but slightly used. *The National Intelligencer* was consulted for the origins of the National Banking System during the Civil War, and the *Vicksburg Daily Whig* for the repudiation movement in Mississippi.

3. The rich pamphlet collection of the Wisconsin Historical Society has been of primary importance in tracing the origins of the National Banking System. In a few cases pamphlets of the Library of Congress have been used.

INDEX

THE RISE OF COMMERCIAL BANKING

An Arno Press Collection

Alcorn, Edgar G. **The Duties and Liabilities of Bank Directors.** 1908

Alhadeff, David A. **Monopoly and Competition in Banking.** 1954

Andersen, Theodore A. **A Century of Banking in Wisconsin.** 1954

Andrew, A. Piatt, Frederick I. Kent, et al. **Banking Problems** 1910

Armstrong, Leroy, and J.O. Denny. **Financial California.** 1916

Balabanis, Homer P. **The American Discount Market.** 1935

Blair, William A. **A Historical Sketch of Banking in North Carolina** *and* Clark, W.A. **The History of the Banking Institutions Organized in South Carolina Prior to 1860.** 2 vols. in one. 1899/1922

Bolles, Albert S. **The National Bank Act and Its Judicial Meaning.** 1892

Bolles, Albert S. **Practical Banking.** 1884

Caldwell, Stephen A. **A Banking History of Louisiana.** 1935

Cannon, James G. **Clearing-Houses.** 1908

Cartinhour, Gaines T. **Branch, Group and Chain Banking** *and* Westerfield, Ray B. **Historical Survey of Branch Banking in the United States.** 2 vols. in one. 1931/1939

Chapman, John M., and Ray B. Westerfield. **Branch Banking.** 1942

Cleaveland, John. **The Banking System of the State of New York.** 1864

Conway, Thomas Jr., and Ernest M. Patterson. **The Operation of the New Bank Act.** 1914

Davis, A.M. **The Origin of the National Banking System.** 1910

Dawes, Charles G. **The Banking System of the United States and Its Relation to the Money and Business of the Country.** 1894

Dewey, Davis, and Martin Shugrue. **Banking and Credit.** 1922

Duke, Basil W. **History of the Bank of Kentucky, 1792-1895.** 1895

Dunbar, Charles F. **Chapters on the Theory and History of Banking.** 1891

Finney, Katherine. **Interbank Deposits.** 1958

Fiske, Amos K. **The Modern Bank.** 1904

Foulke, Roy A. **The Commercial Paper Market.** 1931

Helderman, Leonard C. **National and State Banks.** 1931

Hinchman, T.H. **Banks and Banking in Michigan.** 1887

History of the Chemical Bank 1823-1913. 1913

Hubert, Philip G., Jr. **The Merchants' National Bank of the City of New York.** 1903

Hull, Walter, ed. **Practical Problems in Banking and Currency.** 1907

Hunt, Pearson. **Portfolio Policies of Commercial Banks in the United States 1920-1939.** 1940

Jacoby, Neil, and Raymond Saulnier. **Business Finance and Banking.** 1947

Kane, Thomas P. **The Romance and Tragedy of Banking.** 1923

Kemmerer, Edwin W. **Seasonal Variations in the Relative Demand for Money and Capital in the United States.** 1910

Kniffin, William H., Jr. **American Banking Practice.** 1921

Kniffin, William H., Jr. **Commercial Banking.** 2 vols. 1923

Kniffin, William H., Jr. **The Practical Work of a Bank.** 1919

Krueger, Leonard B. **History of Commerical Banking in Wisconsin.** 1933

Langston, L.H. **Practical Bank Operation.** 2 vols. 1921

Laughlin, J. Laurence, ed. **Banking Reform.** 1912

Macaulay, Frederick R. **Some Theoretical Problems Suggested by the Movements of Interest Rates, Bond Yields and Stock Prices in the United States Since 1856.** 1938

Mitchell, Waldo F. **The Uses of Bank Funds.** 1925

Nadler, Marcus, and Jules I. Bogen. **The Banking Crisis.** 1933

National Industrial Conference Board. **The Banking Situation in the United States.** 1932

Noyes, Alexander D. **Forty Years of American Finance.** 1898/1909

Patten, Claudius B. **The Methods and Machinery of Practical Banking.** 1894

Peterson, Jaffray, compiler. **Sixty-five Years of Progress and a Record of New York City Banks.** 1935

Phillips, Chester A. **Bank Credit.** 1920

Powlison, Keith. **Profits of the National Banks.** 1931

Preston, Howard H. **History of Banking in Iowa.** 1922

Scott, William A. **Money and Banking.** 1910

Stevenson, Russell A., ed. **A Type Study of American Banking.** 1934

Thomas, Rollin G. **The Development of State Banks in Chicago** (Doctoral Dissertation, University of Chicago, 1930). 1980

U.S. Comptroller of the Currency. **Federal Laws Affecting National Banks.** 1936

Watkins, Leonard L. **Bankers' Balances.** 1929

Watkins, Leonard L. **Commercial Banking Reform in the United States.** 1938

Westerfield, Ray B. **Banking Principles and Practice.** 1924

Willis, H. Parker. **American Banking.** 1916

Wright, Benjamin C. **Banking in California 1849-1910.** 1910

Wright, Ivan. **Bank Credit and Agriculture.** 1922